FORBIDDEN LEGO

BUILD THE MODELS YOUR PARENTS WARNED YOU AGAINST!

ULRIK PILEGAARD & MIKE DOOLEY

NO STARCH PRESS

3 4 5 6 7 8 9 10 – 09 08

No Starch Press and the No Starch Press logo are registered trademarks of No Starch Press, Inc. Other product and company names mentioned herein may be the trademarks of their respective owners. Rather than use a trademark symbol with every occurrence of a trademarked name, we are using the names only in an editorial fashion and to the benefit of the trademark owner, with no intention of infringement of the trademark.

Publisher: William Pollock
Managing Editor: Elizabeth Campbell
Cover and Interior Design: Ulrik Pilegaard
Developmental Editor: William Pollock
Copyeditor: Megan Dunchak
Compositor: Octopod Studios
Proofreader: Elizabeth Campbell

For information on book distributors or translations, please contact No Starch Press, Inc. directly:

No Starch Press, Inc.
555 De Haro Street, Suite 250, San Francisco, CA 94107
phone: 415.863.9900; fax: 415.863.9950; info@nostarch.com; http://www.nostarch.com

The information in this book is distributed on an "As Is" basis, without warranty. While every precaution has been taken in the preparation of this work, neither the author nor No Starch Press, Inc. Shall have any liability to any person or entity with respect to any loss or damage caused or alleged to be caused directly or indirectly by the information contained in it.

Library of Congress Cataloging-in-Publication Data

Pilegaard, Ulrik.
  Forbidden LEGO : build the models your parents warned you against / Ulrik Pilegaard and Mike Dooley.
       p. cm.
  Includes index.
  ISBN-13: 978-1-59327-137-4
  ISBN-10: 1-59327-137-9
  1. LEGO toys. I. Dooley, Mike. II. Title.
TS2301.T7P463 2007
688.7'25--dc22
                                                          2006026363

Printed in China

TABLE OF CONTENTS

INTRODUCTION

This book was developed by two people who came to the LEGO Group from very different backgrounds but left sharing a common perspective and a desire to share their experience with others.

ABOUT ULRIK

Ulrik Pilegaard is the chief author and designer of all the models and illustrations in this book. A Dane, Ulrik grew up in LEGO's homeland, a one hour drive from the corporate and spiritual center of LEGO in Billund, Denmark (see Figure 1). He was surrounded by LEGO throughout his childhood.

Figure 1: Location of Billund, Denmark

There are LEGO products in nearly every family's home in Denmark, as well as in the windows of every toy store. In fact, the idea of LEGO itself is intertwined with Danish culture and psyche. Walk the streets of the small towns in Denmark and sometimes you might feel like you are in a mini LEGO world—everything looks LEGO, down to the types of windows and the trademark colors that cover the walls, roofs, and doors. It's sometimes hard to tell whether the buildings are modeled after LEGO sets or LEGO sets are modeled after the buildings. Turn the corner and you might see a gas station with a garage; you'll wonder if it was inspired by LEGO designs or the reverse. This is truly the world of LEGO.

LEGO TECHNIC

When Ulrik was seven years old, he graduated to LEGO TECHNIC. At the time, LEGO TECHNIC was the ultimate expression of LEGO with gears, beams, axles, wheels, and even motors that let children build far beyond the limits of the square and rectangular "System" bricks. Ulrik acquired his first LEGO TECHNIC model, Tractor Art (#851), in 1978. He got the Auto Chassis (# 853) on his birthday in 1979, and on and on, through models #855, #856, #8845, #8846, and beyond.

DANISH DESIGN

Ulrik was also exposed to the pervasive Danish fascination with design: a simple, understated, always graceful, and creative approach to design that is present in everything from living room chairs and hi-fi stereos to salt and pepper shakers.

Ulrik went on to to study design, and he worked as an illustrator and layout editor for a Danish advertising company. But in 1995, he read a job posting from LEGO for a product designer.

He got the job. A Danish boy's dream had come true—Ulrik was a Product Designer for LEGO TECHNIC. He would get to work inside the secret world of LEGO (see Figure 2).

ABOUT MIKE

On the other hand, Mike Dooley, the co-author of this book, was born in the United States. He didn't make it to Denmark until he was hired by LEGO, and although he played with LEGO as a kid, too, he never went beyond the "System" bricks.

Before coming to LEGO, Mike was an MBA working in software marketing in Northern California. A friend and former co-worker recruited Mike to LEGO to help launch a new robotics product line called LEGO MIND-STORMS.

MINDSTORMS BRAINSTORMS

In January 1998, Mike and his team members were gathered around a table at the LEGO headquarters in Billund. Their eyes were focused on an odd looking contraption made

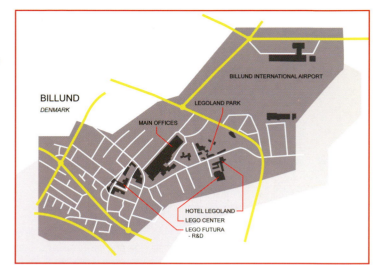

Figure 2: Organization of LEGO Headquarters

of LEGO motors, beams, gears, and a variety of other plastic parts. The model was a proto-type for a new robotics kit being designed for kids ages eight and older. This particular model was intended to be the fourth and final project that kids could build with the kit. The first three models included an insect-like robot called "The Bug," a robotic basketball hoop called "The Hoop-o-bot," and a light sensitive alarm called "Intruder Alarm" that would launch a LEGO "dart" and sound an alarm when someone crossed its electric beam. The fourth model never really had a name. People in the United States would call it a Rube Goldberg type of invention—an elaborate mechanical device that performed many complicated steps in order to do something very simple.

Basically, the fourth model was an over-engineered ball dispenser. A person could load about three ping-pong sized balls into a vertical stack mounted at the top of the model, and a small arm at the base of the stack would rotate and eject one ball at a time from the bottom of the stack. From there, the ball would roll down a track that wound around the outside of the model. At the end of the track, the ball would fall into a paddle wheel that would catch it and carry it on the wheel before letting it roll out onto the table.

Mike thought it would be really cool to have the ball fall into a third mechanism like a catapult, which could do something useful like throw the ball to someone from the other side of a ping-pong table, like an automatic serving machine. But by this point, the project had already run over budget for building elements that could go into the set, and LEGO "rules" discouraged putting things like a catapult in a product. (You'll learn more about these "rules" a bit later.)

Mike also learned that he couldn't put just anything into a LEGO product. If he wanted to include a part that LEGO didn't make (like a ping-pong ball), LEGO had to clear the component. For this product, the team chose to use Nerf-like yellow foam balls, which worked well for the Hoop-o-bot and which LEGO already had on its approved list. Unfortunately, the uneven texture of the foam balls added a lot of friction, which made it harder to dispense them from the stack. Sometimes the balls would jam up in the stack; other times two would get stuck together and come out at the same time. (You'll encounter a similar problem when you try to move objects like candy through machines built out of LEGO: That slick ABS plastic finish just doesn't mix well with sugar coating.)

PROBLEM SOLVED!

LEGO designers are nothing if they're not inventors, and the lead model designer on the team had come up with a solution to the problem. He created a simple rotating arm that would turn clockwise like a turntable. The arm would come in through a horizontal slit in the base of the stack, contact the midpoint of the ball, and slowly but forcefully push it out through an opening on the opposite side of the stack. The second ball in the stack would gradually descend as the first ball was pushed out, with the back side of the rotating arm serving as an extra brace on the second ball to block it from rolling through the opening before it fell to the bottom of the stack. Two LEGO slanted roof bricks at the base of the stack created a small cradle that held the ball in place once the arm cleared the stack.

After about 15 seconds, the arm would rotate all the way around and repeat the process, pushing the second ball slightly up over the cradle and out of the stack, and lowering the third ball into place. The process would continue as long as there were balls in the stack.

The team watched as the lead designer demonstrated his contraption, which worked perfectly time and time again. They were particularly impressed by the fact that the rotating arm was built almost entirely of parts already used in the other three models, which meant that kids could build it using the same set.

The mechanism for driving the swing arm was a crucial part of the cost savings. The lead designer had simplified the design by re-using a worm gear assembly that was already part of the Intruder Alarm. The worm gear assembly was a combination of gears and axles housed in a special LEGO block that held them together. It would gear the small, 9V LEGO motor's speed by a factor of 24 to 1 to create the very slow but steady motion needed for the arm. The assembly also created a lot of torque, which was perfect for applying just the right amount of pressure for pushing the ball out of the stack. In fact, the force was so strong, it was actually hard to stop the arm from turning using your hand.

THE UNINTENTIONAL PROJECTILE LAUNCHER

The team reveled in this latest achievement of creativity and engineering, one of those small milestones designers celebrate when they overcome a design problem that has been troubling them for days. But unfortunately, Mike had to ruin the celebration—it was those pesky LEGO rules again. (It is the toy business, after all, and there are such things as product liability.) Mike asked one of those dreaded "what if" questions: "What if the child ran the motor in reverse?" The lead designer reset the machine and turned the motor on in reverse.

Until this point, Mike hadn't realized just how much kinetic energy a simple motor and plastic worm gear could store. With the motor running in reverse, the rotating arm ran in the opposite direction, traveling back to where it had pushed out the first ball. But the second ball was still in the stack, and it blocked the arm from passing through the slit it had originally entered. Stalled, the arm squeezed tightly against the middle of the foam ball and pinned the ball against the inside of the stack, while the motor continued to crank the axles and gears.

The arm slowed as it compressed the last millimeter it could get out of the ball, and for a brief moment, it appeared to stop. But then the team heard the sound of creaking plastic as the structure of the model started to warp. The base of the stack began to twist and bow. The creaking became louder and the model more distorted. Suddenly, with a loud pop, one of the LEGO TECHNIC beams gave way and shot straight out at an incredible speed.

The beam flew a good 15 feet before smacking into the wall. With the beam gone, the arm, with some dangling LEGO elements, continued its rotation and pushed the ball along through what was now a much wider opening in the stack. The model returned to its original shape, minus a few pieces. This was not good.

Everyone on the team laughed, but they knew that they could not go forward with this design. The problem was not with the durability of the model; none of the LEGO parts were damaged, and it was easy to put the dislodged pieces back into their original position. (In fact, in their 12 years of combined experience working with LEGO robots, Ulrik and Mike have never seen a plastic LEGO element actually break or even crack under normal wear and tear.) The problem was that the team had unintentionally turned their innocent Rube Goldberg device into a formidable projectile launcher. Had they been building the invention for themselves, they would have been happy with the new feature; they probably would have said something in Danish equivalent to "cool" and then gone out to think of creative ways to use it over a few beers.

THE OFFICIAL SAFETY TEST

The official LEGO safety test for toys with projectiles involves a piece of plastic kitchen wrap stretched across an open frame. The tester fires a projectile, like a spring-loaded toy dart, at the plastic wrap. The plastic wrap is meant to predict potential damage to the surface of a child's eye. If the projectile breaks the plastic or tears any sort of hole in it, the part is considered unsafe, and the designer has to reduce the force of the mechanism firing the projectile, redesign the projectile so that it distributes its force across a wider area of impact, or remove the projectile from the toy altogether. In the case of the Rube Goldberg device, the beam probably would have punched a two-inch hole in the plastic.

On a project several years back, Ulrik and his team had been trying to create a robotic vehicle that would eject a LEGO TECHNIC action figure when a target on the vehicle was hit a certain number of times. The team had designed the model so that the action figure would not have enough force to break the plastic wrap in the safety test, but the ejection seat was forbidden anyway because a child could put something else in the seat other than the TECHNIC action figure—such as a LEGO brick, a rock, or some other foreign object—and then use the seat to launch that object. Under this scenario, the safety test with the plastic wrap had to apply to *anything* that could fit in the launcher.

Ulrik's team overcame this problem by designing their model to have a self-contained sub-assembly as part of the launching mechanism, almost like a key, so that the model could not eject anything other than the TECHNIC action figure. They constructed the model so that the whole cockpit, with the TECHNIC figure inside, was thrown off the model.

However, they weren't building the model for themselves; it was for kids. And making models that threw random pieces at high speeds was against the rules—falling somewhere under the "you could poke someone's eye out doing that" general clause. (Well, the shooting LEGO beam was probably not forceful enough to really poke out someone's eyes, but it could do some damage, and it definitely exceeded the official speed limit for LEGO pieces.)

THE LAND OF FORBIDDEN LEGO

Some of the best LEGO creations that Ulrik and Mike saw were ones that could never pass all of the LEGO rules. Many of those cool models would just disappear or be cannibalized for parts.

But not all the forbidden ideas are lost. There is a special place for them in Billund, nestled in among the maze of LEGO buildings that house the many marketing and product development groups.

In the basement, tucked away at the far end of a catacomb-like room, is a long row of gray metal shelves. The shelves look like something more appropriate for the archive section of a college library or the legal records department of a large corporation. They are tightly packed on a rolling track with little space between the sets of shelves, but there is a button that makes the shelves part, creating an aisle.

Nearly every shelf is filled with LEGO models from past projects. Most aren't models from actual commercial products but are mock-ups for early ideas and concepts that never saw the light of day.

This is the LEGO equivalent of the Land of Misfit Toys. Some models are a bit damaged and others are missing a few parts, but most have managed to keep their identity. Many are wild by LEGO standards, using prototype parts that didn't exist within the system; some are based entirely on their own custom construction system.

Together, this collection of models represents dreams that never came to be. The designers keep the models here for inspiration and to use as brainstorming tools. Every so often, designers will come down to revisit an old idea for a new product or examine the way some builder had approached a complex design 10 years ago. We think the builders keep the models around for sentimental reasons, as well—as a way to connect with the creative energy and spirit that each model has stored inside it.

WHY THIS BOOK?

We chose to write this book to share a bit of the raw energy and inventiveness we experienced at LEGO but that we could never fully express in our products. This is not meant to be a criticism of LEGO or its products in any way. It is the toy *business*, and it's not easy to sell such an open-ended array of products to millions of kids.

We truly believe that LEGO does what it does with more heart, soul, and care than any other company in the world. The LEGO process yields great products, which get better and better.

Forbidden LEGO is about taking advantage of the creative freedom available to those of us outside the company. Our goal is to encourage you to use that freedom to unleash an extra bit of creative energy to build great and wonderful things.

In the following chapters, you'll find the ghosts of forbidden ideas materialized, along with some new ideas that we could never even consider carrying out while employed by LEGO. But please don't stop after you've built these models. Our hope is that as you learn how we create, you will begin to think of ways to master, bend, and break the rules yourself, making the most of LEGO and your imagination. And perhaps you too will have the pleasure of joining the LEGO Company and visiting the real land of Forbidden LEGO. You will find our ghosts there.

In memory of all the LEGO toys that never were,
and in anticipation of those yet to come,
build great things, create, and enjoy.

Med venlig hilsen,
(Kindest regards,)

Ulrik Pilegaard *and* **Mike Dooley**

HOW TO BUILD GREAT THINGS

People are always asking LEGO master builders where they come up with all the great new models and products. This is especially true with the more advanced LEGO TECHNIC and MIND-STORMS products, which amaze people with what a bunch of plastic pieces can do. For example, take a look at the independent suspension of the TECHNIC Super Car (#8448) or the four-legged walking motion of the AT-AT from the *Star Wars* Dark Side Developer Kit (#9754). From an outsider's point of view, coming up with mechanisms like these can seem very daunting, if not impossible.

HOW WE BUILD AT LEGO

LEGO builders start with an empty table, some information about the target audience for their product, the purpose of the product, and a budget (basically, how much the parts required for the final model should cost). Of course, the builders at LEGO do have a significant advantage over you or me: They have a virtually endless supply of almost every LEGO piece ever created right at their fingertips, and they can have custom parts designed and fabricated in a matter of days if they can't quite get something to fit together. And on top of all that, they have years of practice and training under other master builders who have shared the secrets of the LEGO trade that they have acquired over decades.

Sounds like it should be easy, doesn't it? You might think that coming up with the ideas, building the prototypes, and deciding on the models that will go into a set is the hardest part about creating a new toy at LEGO. However, most of the work is in the constant refining, optimizing, and checking for quality and cost. And, of course, at all points, the builders need to make sure the product they're creating satisfies the LEGO rules.

The job of the master builder requires considerable patience and compromise, especially when balancing the fun and freedom of creating new toys with the reality of putting a final product on store shelves.

THE EARLY STAGES

The early stages of designing a project are great ones because there are so few constraints. The designers brainstorm and configure their models in whatever way works.

It's great fun to make trips to the hardware-store-sized central LEGO stock room where designers can walk down aisle after aisle and put their hands in bins that appear to offer a bottomless supply of pieces for use in new creations. Every LEGO block is available in every approved color.

The designers build some truly incredible things with the wide variety of available LEGO pieces. A team of designers will often work on the same idea for several weeks, gathered around a table, with each person adding some new bit or making a small change to make the model even better.

During this process, the designers work with marketing managers to ensure that the product will fit what customers want, even when the marketing managers aren't exactly sure what that is. In a company as big as LEGO, with divisions around the world, it can take some time to get everyone's feedback. Feedback may come from leading retailers in different countries or from the third-parties behind licenses like Harry Potter and *Star Wars*, who have a lot to say about what is right and wrong with a product.

Final feedback comes when a product is put in front of kids, especially when that product represents a new, unprecedented concept for LEGO.

BACK TO EARTH

The exploratory phase can go on for months, depending on the project, but the exploration does need to move forward. Once exploration ends, the team has a wonderful set of models that look like they are just begging for kids to play with them. However, the work really intensifies when the designers have to think about how to get these wonderful inventions through LEGO's system control so that kids *can* eventually play with them.

First and foremost, there is the budget. The designers add up the cost of all of the pieces of each of the models to find the raw unit cost of the product. The number they come up with is usually twice what the product manager has budgeted, and the cooler models are generally even further out of range.

DURABILITY, ASSEMBLY, AND CORRECTNESS

Then the designers begin the rebuilding and redesigning stage. They go back and try to recreate the great model that impressed everyone—this time, using fewer and cheaper pieces. This can be a very tedious process, because each of up to several hundred parts has to be tracked and figured into the cost with each new interaction of the model.

During this stage, the designers are also thinking about model durability, ease of assembly, and correctness of design.

LEGO has a great deal of experience with durability, especially when it concerns how parts wear over time or under different environmental conditions. The company has sets of internal rules about the "right" way to build, which means designing models that will stay in perfect shape even if a kid leaves them on the windowsill exposed to the sun for months.

When considering ease of assembly, the designers try to imagine creating a set of building instructions to go along with each product, with a goal of ensuring that the intricate mechanisms they have created will be easy to explain through a sequence of simple visual steps.

Finally, the designers have to make sure that the LEGO "math" adds up: each piece in the complex three-dimensional form must conform to the precise spacing defined by the module system of measurement (1 module is 8 mm, or as wide as a 1 stud brick). This goes beyond simply counting up modules; the designer must check every place that gears meet or an axle fits into the socket of an angle joint and even note how much a rubber band is stretched. All of the pieces are designed to work perfectly together when placed in the right positions, and the rule-keepers frown and shake their heads at any improvisations that violate the system.

THE HERO MODEL

If a kit contains more than one model, as with MINDSTORMS kits, the designers will begin by redesigning the hero model first. The *hero model* is the LEGO equivalent of the money shot. It's the model every kid wants to build first and the one the sales and marketing people will plaster on posters, ads, and boxes. The designers begin with the hero model because it is the most important model in the set and the one they need to make sure they can build without going over their parts budget.

Once the designers settle on a version of the hero model that satisfies everyone's criteria, they look at how they can use mostly the same pieces and a minimum of extra ones to build the remaining models. With product kits that contain several models, like the Dark Side Developer Kit (#9754) and Droid Developer Kit (#9748), this is an extremely grueling process. Often, in order to use as few parts in the complete set as possible, the designers have to change some aspects of the hero model. Sometimes key functions or even entire models are dropped in order to make the piece count.

note: When most people look at two different models in a set, they usually don't realize that the models are built using 90 percent of the same pieces. It's sort of like being able to make each meal in a three-course dinner from a single set of ingredients. (For what it's worth, Taco Bell basically follows the same formula.)

MASTER VERSIONS

Once the designers have optimized the design of all the models in a product and squeezed out the last bit of cost, master versions of the models are submitted to a review process called *Maturing*. During this process, a cadre of model builders creates replicas of the models for evaluation by various internal groups including (during our time at LEGO) the Model Committee. The senior designers on this committee act as a final checkpoint to verify that the models follow all appropriate guidelines for design, durability, ease of assembly, and safety, and that they don't contain anything that might be deemed "un-LEGO."

note: A designer at LEGO once confided to a fellow designer that he used to purposely include small mistakes in the design to give the Committee members something obvious to criticize. This way, the Committee members would feel like they had done their work, the design team could easily fix the models to conform to the Committee's recommendation, and the Committee's attention would be drawn away from some other problematic aspect of the design that would require significant re-working of the model.

BUILDING STEPS

Once the models are approved, their designs are broken down into building steps. In this process, the model is rebuilt in stages, with a few extra pieces added at each stage. Every stage is physically built and glued to its own board for documentation. The boards are then turned over to a Computer Aided Design (CAD) group that creates a computer rendering of each building step, which is then used to create the printed building instructions that are shipped with the final product.

note: This means that if you purchase a LEGO kit with a model that has 127 building steps, there are 127 separate boards with the model in various stages of completion sitting on some shelf in a warehouse in Denmark. This serves as a sort of memorial to all of the work that went into getting that product into your hands.

Having experienced this process several times firsthand, we can assure you that every new LEGO product represents a great achievement that goes well beyond the technology of the building system. The entire organization is designed to take a few fortunate people's dreams and experiences and transform them into a reality that is shared by millions of children around the world.

If you watch a child open a new set of bricks and start building, you may even realize that the ultimate hero in LEGO isn't the model or the designer, it's the builder. It's anyone who has shared in the experience of putting something together, whether by following someone else's lead or by exploring on their own. The energy is very much alive, and the more you participate, the more tangible it becomes.

GREAT DESIGNS START WITH A SIMPLE IDEA

Having a wealth of LEGO pieces, resources, and knowledge all help support the master builder's work, but no idea becomes reality without the consumer. In this regard, the idea is the most important element in any LEGO model—and because anyone can have a great idea, anyone can build a great model. However, the key to being a successful builder is in the way you select and test your LEGO-related ideas. Here are the steps we suggest you follow.

PICK YOUR IDEA

Choose an idea that you are truly passionate about. You have to want this idea to become real and believe that you can make it work. Frequently at LEGO, a single designer with limited experience makes a breakthrough on something that stumped a whole team of seasoned builders because that one designer had a clearer vision for what he wanted to achieve. Driven by a vision like that, you can explore more ways of reaching the goal, instead of simply giving up when faced with a challenge.

TAKE SMALL STEPS

Approach your idea in small steps. Before you can really begin building, you must break down the idea for your invention into its most basic parts. Think of each critical function as a small idea of its own, and then think about how you can test the mechanics of each idea, one at a time.

One good way to break your model into its constituent steps is to begin by quickly building something that does not necessarily look anything like what you want the model to look like, but that satisfies one or more of the key functions that the final model will have to perform. By going through this process for each major function, you quickly discover some of the major design challenges that would only have shown up later when you tried to build the entire model. This approach also lets your mind observe and experience how each function works, as you begin to think about how the system of functions will need to work together.

KEEP YOUR DESIGNS

If you have enough parts, keep your initial designs of the various functions of your model for reference until the model is finished. By holding onto each stage of your work, you can always improve on the original idea and explore new ways of creating the same effect more simply. This approach may well mean that you will have to rebuild some subassemblies or even the entire model several times, but that's what makes great LEGO models!

DON'T GET STUCK

Don't get stuck on one thing. The more flexible you are, the more creative your solution will be. If you can't figure out one or more of the functions of your invention, work on a different function. Once you've had some success there, return to the function that stumped you earlier. To quote a MINDSTORMS training mission for kids, "Be a mover, not a stopper." If you just can't resolve a design problem no matter how you try, consider redefining part or all of the problem. There is always more than one right way to do something with LEGO; that's simply the nature of the building system.

BE OPEN

Be open to new ideas as they come along. Sometimes you will discover that the greatest and most original ideas appear while you are trying to solve an entirely different problem. Be ready to let go of your old goals and ideas if you find better ones along the way.

And don't limit yourself. No rule is sacred in LEGO, especially if it gets in the way of your creativity. Use whatever works for you to make your ideas reality.

A FEW WORDS ON SAFETY

In the grand scheme, there far more hazardous things in the world than playing with LEGO models, even if you don't follow the official LEGO rules. In fact, most things in life are more hazardous than playing with LEGO models, even when playing with them means building the forbidden models in this book.

However, we do stress that this book is intended for *mature* hobbyists. *These projects are not specifically designed with children in mind, and as such, do not conform to toy safety standards.*

While exploring the ideas and projects presented in this book, take reasonable care and adequate precautions. Treat the projects as you would any other personal craft. This means *responsibly* handling small parts, batteries, small motors, electrical circuits, potential flying objects, non-LEGO components, and any tools that you may use to modify standard LEGO pieces.

Although probably the most harmful thing you can do with this book is throw it at someone, we remind you not to use the ideas or projects in this book in any way that could harm you or another living thing. For example, do not shoot your friends or your pets with the Paper Plane Launcher or the High Velocity Automatic Plate Dispenser. In fact, don't aim the models at anyone, even if you think they aren't loaded. Take similar care when using the Candy Coated Catapult. Do not use the catapult to launch a piece of candy at any part of your face, especially your mouth.

note: Trying to launch a piece of candy directly into your mouth is a very good way to make yourself choke!

Overall, just use common sense. If you are seriously lacking in common sense or have a history of household accidents that have led to multiple trips to the emergency room, immediately place this book back on the shelf where you found it and slowly step away. Try finding a less dangerous book in the self-help aisle, and work your way up to this one when you're ready.

PROJECT 1:
PAPER PLANE LAUNCHER (PPL)

THE INSPIRATION

As LEGOLAND has proven for over 40 years, you can build just about anything with LEGO bricks—from buildings and windmills to ships and cable cars. With the launch of LEGO TECHNIC in 1978, it became possible to build mechanical devices that used gears, axles, and motors. Since then, LEGO has been launching new and innovative TECHNIC elements that make it easier and more fun to build whatever you dream of. Yes, even a Paper Plane Launcher.

Like the Candy Coated Catapult and the Ping-Pong Cannon, this model uses non-LEGO parts that either are household items or are readily available in stores. It's especially fun to build models that incorporate familiar items in unusual, new ways, and it's always amazing when you see what you can build with a bunch of plastic parts. Most people can fold a sheet of paper into at least a couple of cool looking planes, and even if your paper airplanes don't fly very well on their own, the PPL will make them soar.

THE DESIGN

Our goal was to make this model as simple as possible without using a motor or batteries. There were three challenges in our design:

1. The first challenge was tightening the rubber band. We succeeded with a gear wheel and added an axle to keep the wheel from rolling back—a technique that has been around for a long time in the LEGO world.

2. The second challenge was creating the launch trigger. The trigger needed to be easy to use and easy to reload. Ulrik came up with a particularly neat mechanism: two L-shaped half beams that hold the rubber band in position while you tighten it by turning the gear wheel ratchet. By suddenly removing the angle beam that the L-shaped half beams are resting against, the half beams rotate and the rubber band is released. Voilà!

3. The third challenge was designing the paper plane holder. In order to ensure that the rubber band that launches the plane is guided to the tail of the plane, the plane must be placed very carefully in between the two rubber bands running back to the trigger. This mechanism holds the plane tightly enough so that it won't release inadvertently if you point the model up or down, but not so tightly that the plane will not launch when the rubber band is released.

LEGO RULES BROKEN

This model would be shot down in seconds at LEGO. Not only are you firing something at a very high speed, but the object being fired is not even a LEGO part.

LEGO usually avoids including non-LEGO pieces as part of a model. One reason is quality control—LEGO has very high standards. The other reason is probably ego maintenance. Designers consider it a cop-out to not build everything out of 100 percent LEGO pieces.

Even if LEGO had decided to create the airplane used in this model, it would probably have chosen to build the frame from standard TECHNIC elements and would have used custom-designed official LEGO fabric-like material for the surface of the wings. LEGO would *not* want to encourage children to construct their own paper airplanes.

NON-LEGO PARTS USED

We used a stock LEGO rubber band from the Dragster set (#8205) to build the model shown here. However, you can use almost any rubber band, as long as it's long enough and you can fasten it to the drum.

Although we attempted to incorporate everyday household items into all the projects in this book, each part in the PPL project could be found in at least one or two LEGO sets. On the other hand, the whole point of this model is to shoot something that is not a LEGO part: a paper airplane.

PAPER PLANE LAUNCHER

5, 4, 3, 2, 1, LIFTOFF!

Okay, maybe we're being a bit dramatic, but it does look cool when you shoot a paper airplane off at speeds the Highway Patrol would ticket you for! Fold another airplane, adjust the wings slightly, and practice precision flying with your friends. The Paper Plane Launcher (PPL) is easy to build, easy to use, and — most importantly — easy to create replacement planes for.

HOW IT WORKS

1. Load the rubber band by wrapping it around the wheel in the front and then around the trigger.

2. Mount your paper airplane by sliding it in between the slots.

3. Wind the rubber band until your face turns red, then pull the trigger! (Since you can wind the rubber band to the point where the launcher actually puts a dent in your airplane, we suggest putting a piece of tape on the back of the airplane to help it handle the initial impact.)

PARTS LIST

PAPER PLANE LAUNCHER

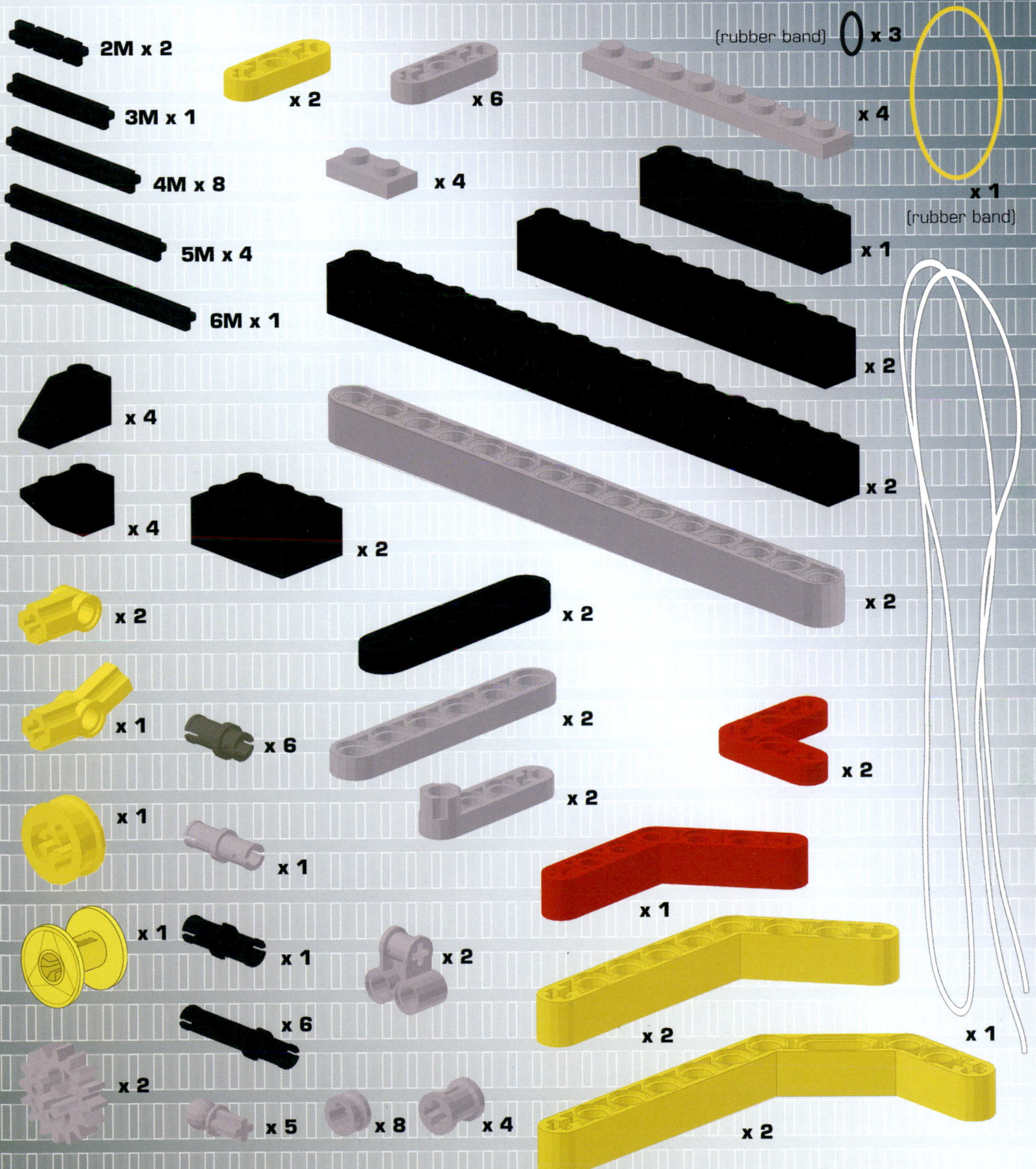
2M x 2
3M x 1
4M x 8
5M x 4
6M x 1
x 2
x 6
x 4
x 4
(rubber band) x 3
x 1
(rubber band)
x 1
x 2
x 2
x 4
x 4
x 2
x 2
x 2
x 2
x 1
x 6
x 2
x 2
x 2
x 1
x 1
x 1
x 1
x 1
x 2
x 2
x 1
x 6
x 2
x 5
x 8
x 4
x 2

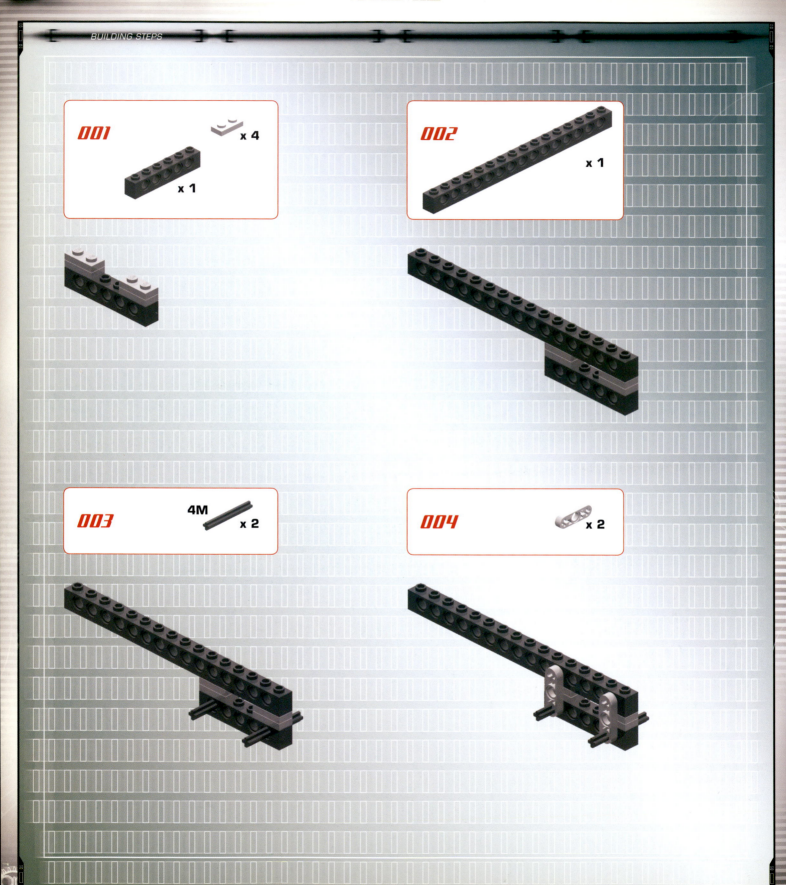

001 x 4 x 1

002 x 1

003 4M x 2

004 x 2

005

x 2

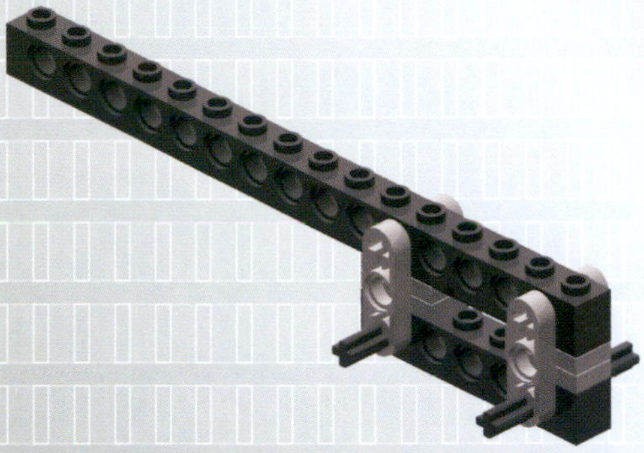

006

2M

x 1

4M

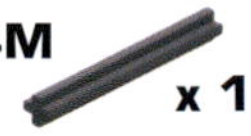

x 1

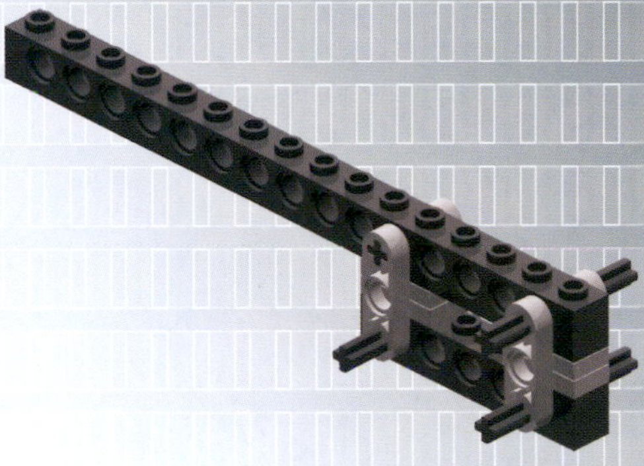

007

6M

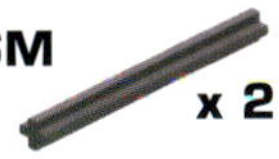

x 2

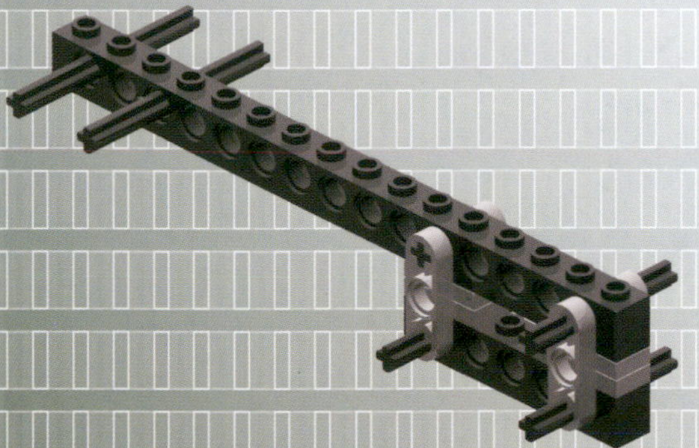

008

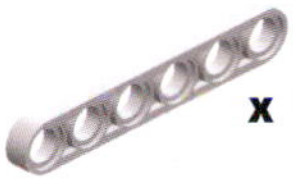

x 2

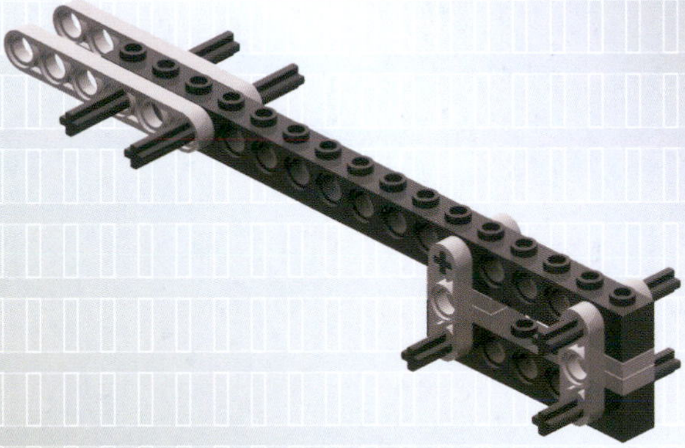

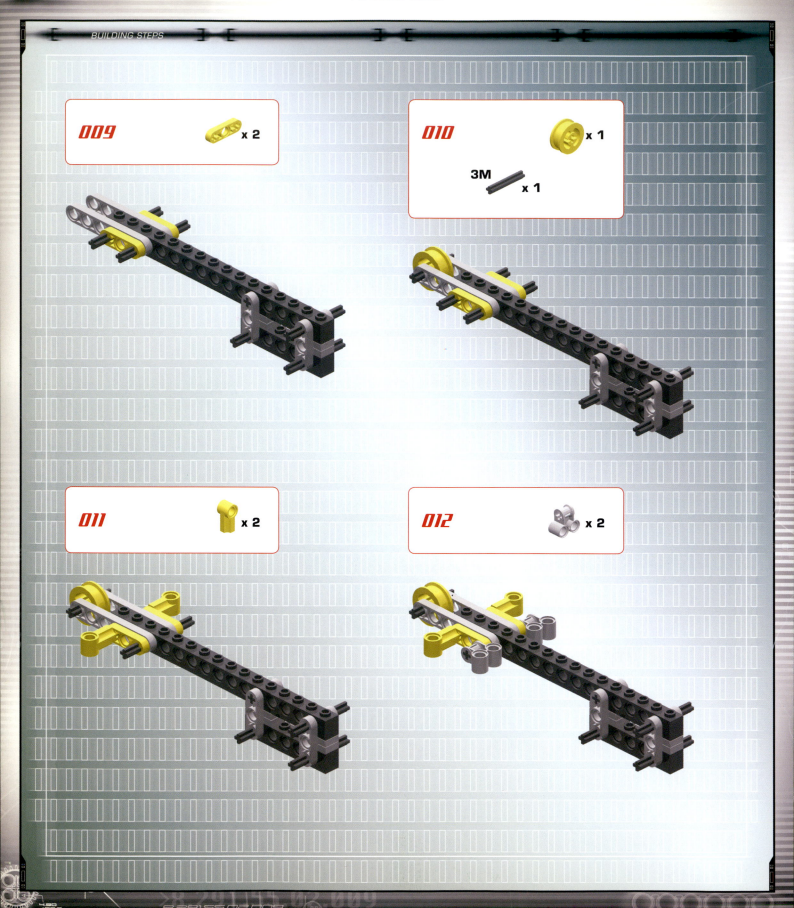

009   x 2

010   x 1
3M   x 1

011   x 2

012   x 2

013 x 2

014

x 1

x 1 4M x 1

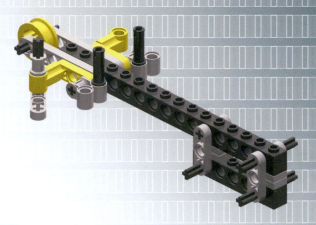

015

x 1

x 1 4M x 1

016 x 2

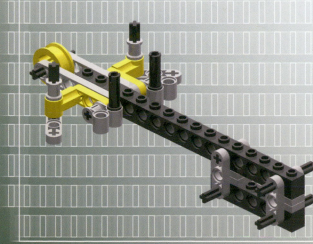

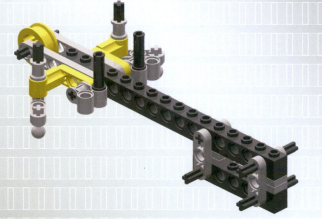

BUILDING STEPS

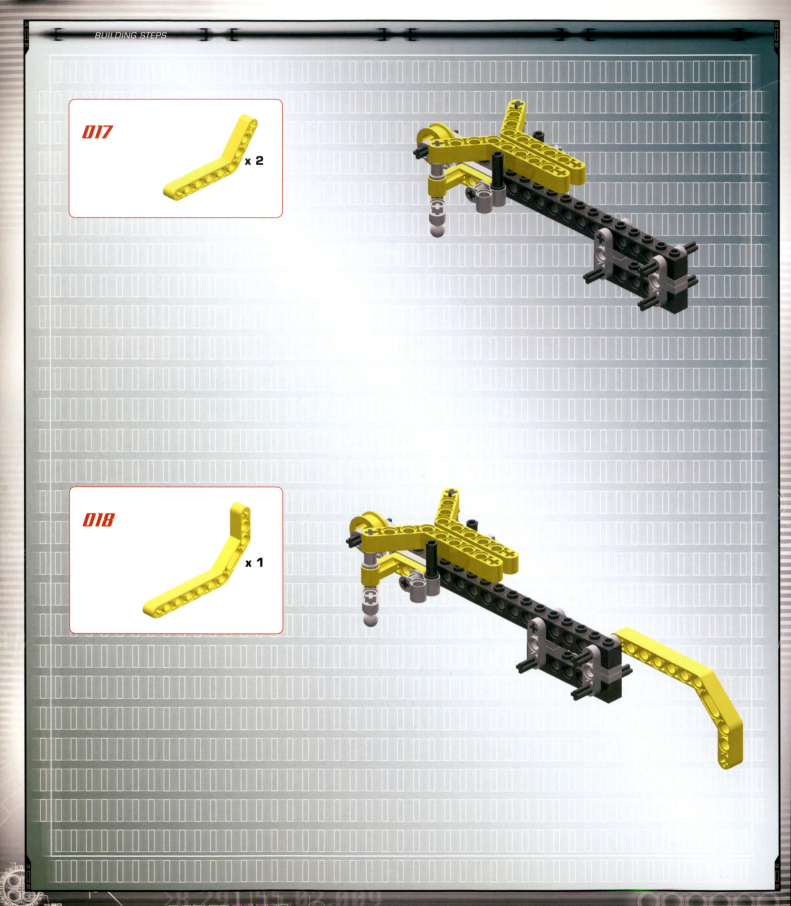

017

x 2

018

x 1

019

4M

x 1

x 1

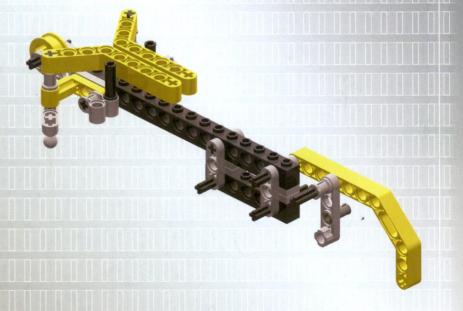

020

x 1

x 1

021 x 2
x 1

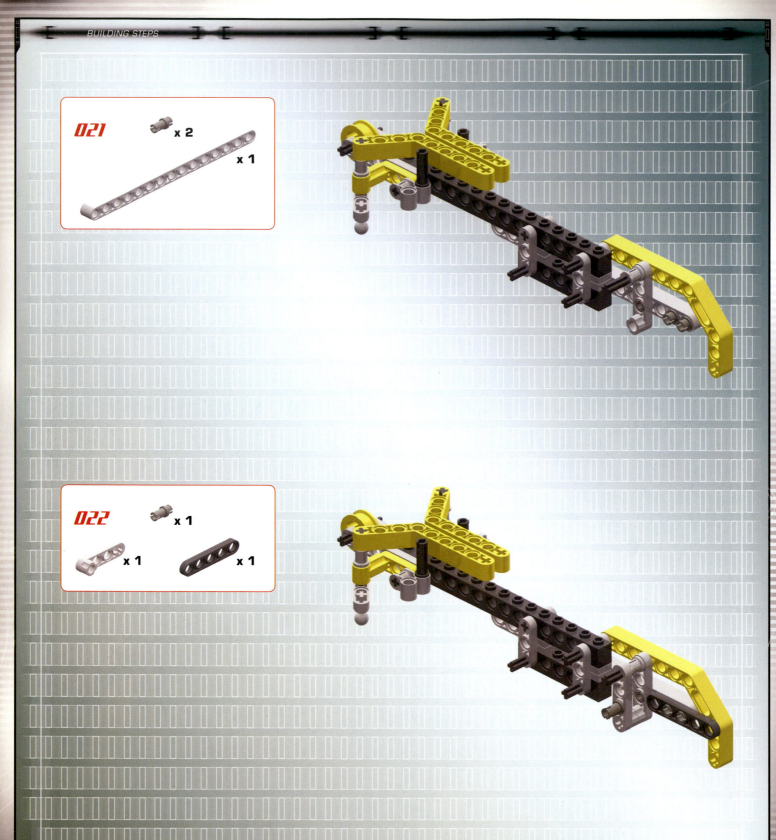

022 x 1
x 1
x 1

023
4M x 1
x 1

024
4M x 1
x 2

025
x 2

026
x 1

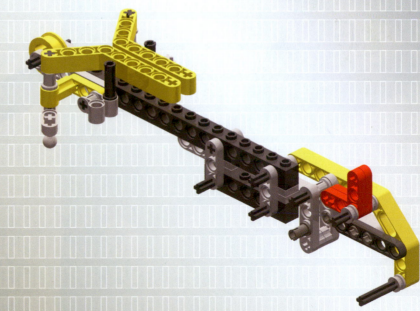

027   x 3

x 1

028   x 2

029   x 4

030   x 4

031

 x 2

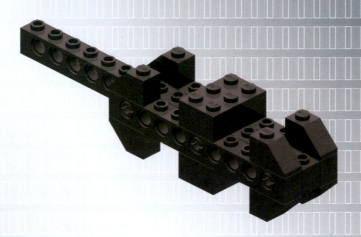

032

 x 4

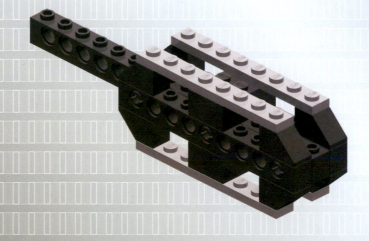

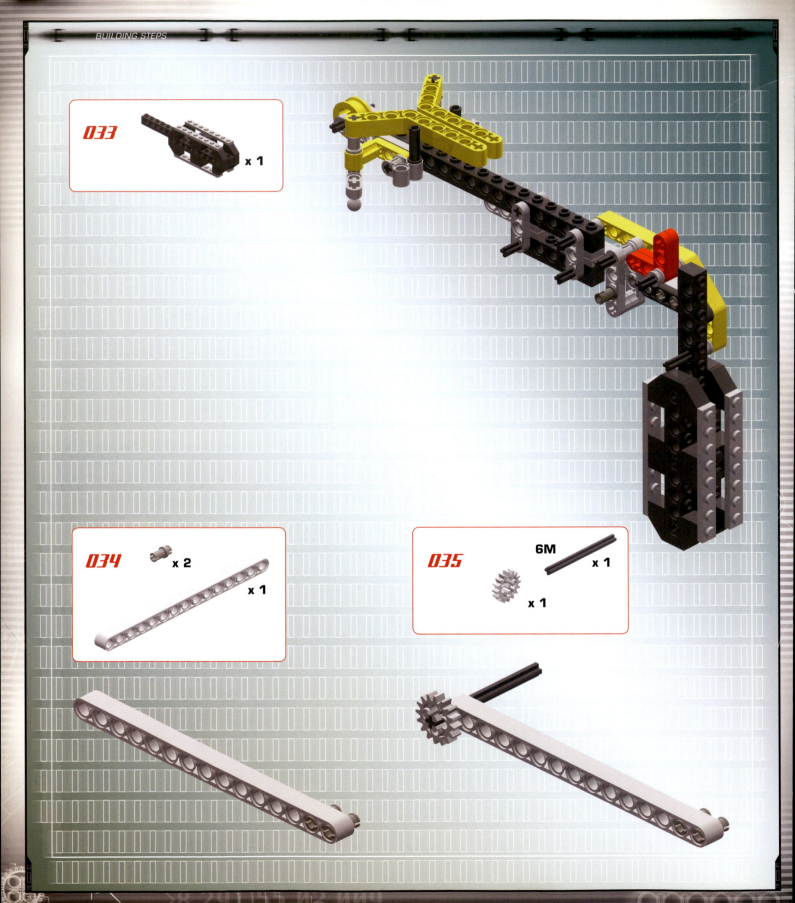

033 x 1

034 x 2 x 1

035 6M x 1 x 1

036

x 1

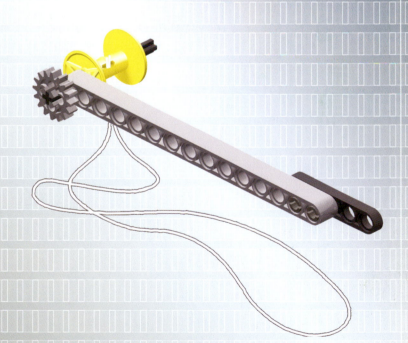

037

x 1

x 1

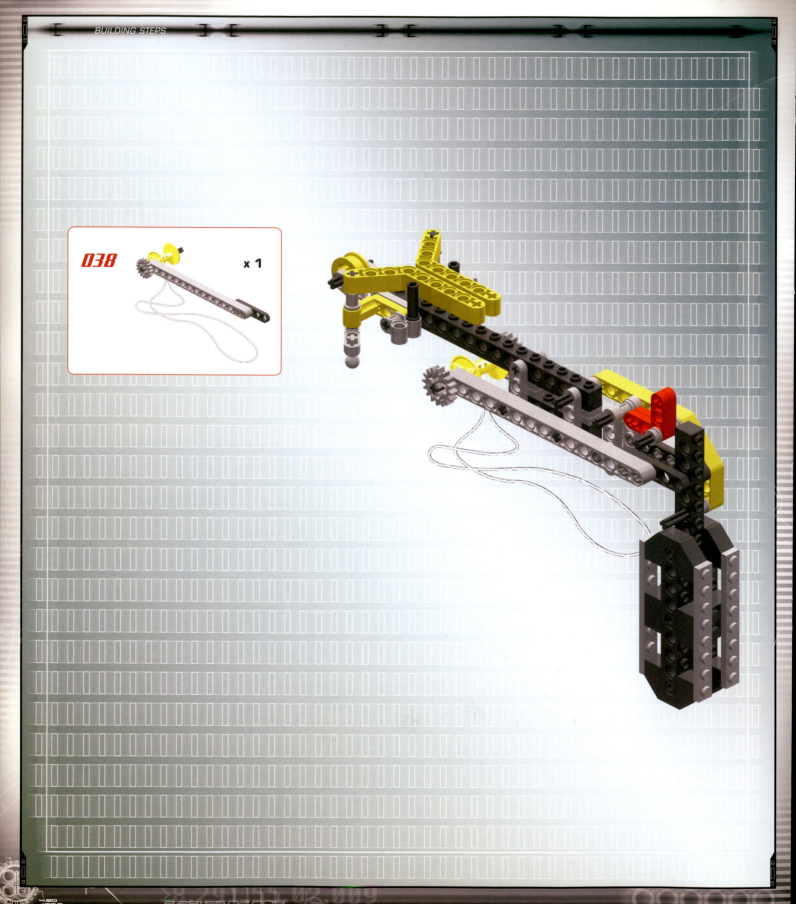

038 x 1

039 . 🔩 x 1

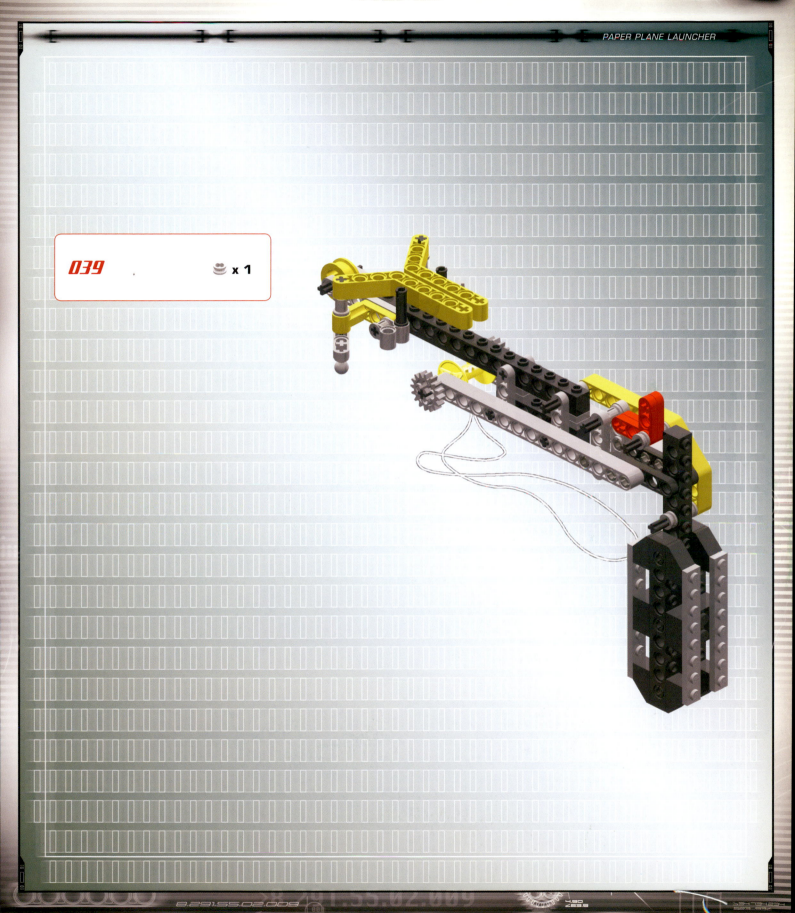

040

x 1

041

5M x 1

x 2

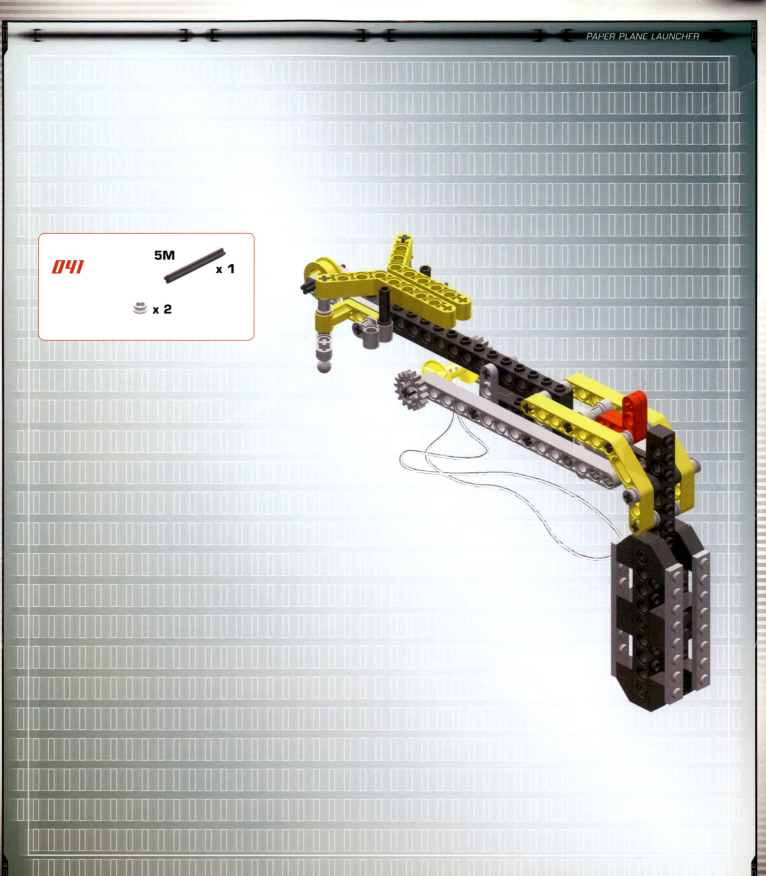

042

x 2

5M

x 1

x 1

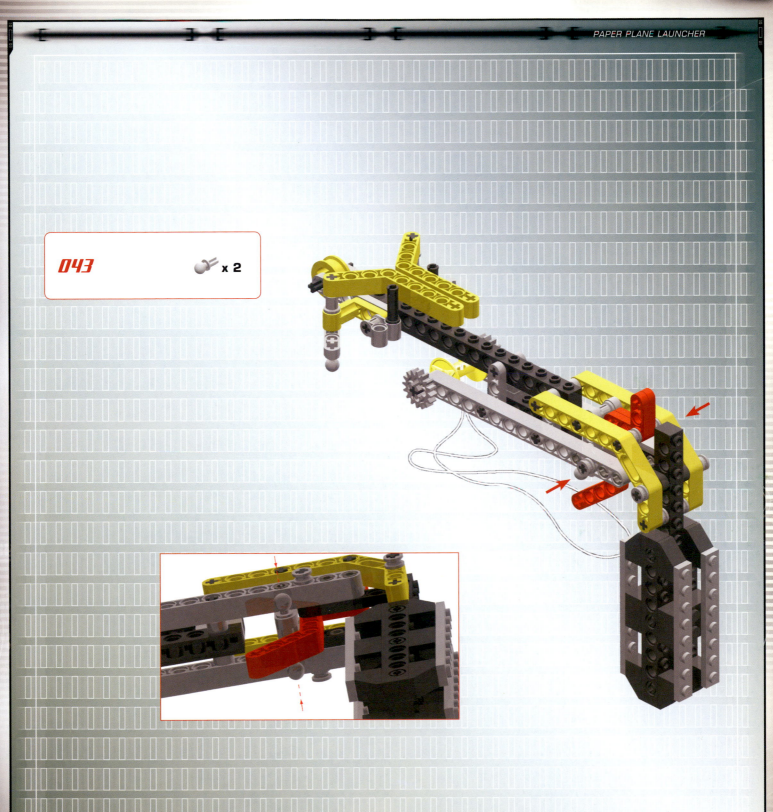

043 x 2

044

x 1

x 1

045

x 1

x 1 **2M** x 1

046

x 1

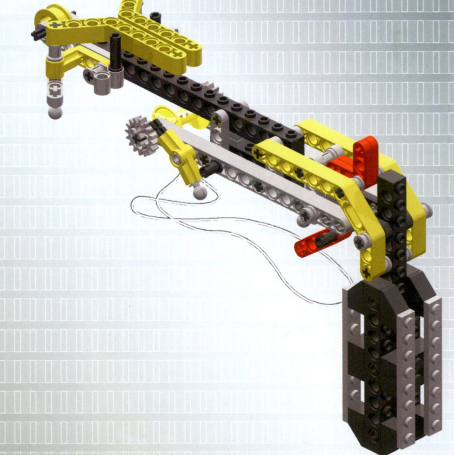

047

x 1

(rubber band)

x 3

(rubber band)

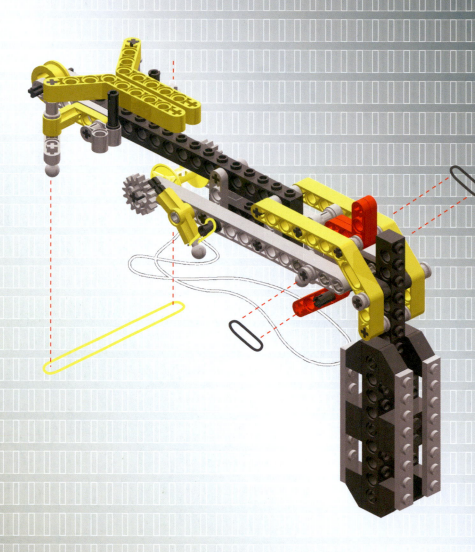

PROJECT 2:
CANDY COATED CATAPULT (CCC)

THE INSPIRATION

For as long as we have known each other, Mike has talked about building "a candy machine." His dream was to sit on his couch watching TV, press a button on his trusty LEGO MINDSTORMS remote control, and have a machine on a table launch a piece of candy across the room and into his lap.

note: *Warning: Mike used to talk a lot about (and do a lot of) eating candy, sitting on couches, and watching TV, but then he had to go on a serious diet and exercise program after leaving LEGO.*

Having to comply with the LEGO rules meant we could not make the ultimate candy catapult of Big Mike's dreams. As a small consolation, we and the MINDSTORMS development group did put a candy dispenser into the Robotics Invention System 2.0 set (#3804) as a Pro-level challenge. This invention would dispense one piece of candy at a time from a stack, scan the color of each piece as it came out, and use a conveyor belt on a turntable to sort the different colored pieces into separate piles. This was a nice trick, but our true goal was always to create something that could make candy fly. That goal is now realized in the CCC.

THE DESIGN

For this model to work, a lot of energy needs to be released at once, but in a consistent and controlled manner. While this type of mechanism can be built from many LEGO pieces like beams, plates, springs, rubber bands, and gears, Ulrik discovered a much more elegant approach: the common plastic spoon.

note: *A plastic spork may be used as a substitute if you happen to be out of spoons.*

The plastic spoon turns out to be close to perfect for use in the CCC because it is stiff, yet flexible enough to bend several degrees without breaking. This characteristic has been proven for decades by kids launching food volleys in school lunchrooms across the globe. By way of comparison, if you have built even just a little bit with LEGO, you know that almost all of the standard ABS plastic elements are far too rigid to provide this type of flexibility.

The rounded part of the spoon provides a natural form for holding most standard-sized pieces of candy. Also, plastic spoons are cheap, available in large quantities, and suitable for many purposes, such as eating ice cream while you are building your candy-catapulting machine. Based on first hand experience, we know that if you don't satisfy your appetite in other ways, you may find yourself eating your entire stock of candy projectiles before your model is complete.

When it came time to build, the first thing we needed to do was design a locking mechanism for the plastic spoon. Once completed, the locking assembly prototype served as a testing device for determining which gear ratio we would need in order to make a standard LEGO motor flick the spoon. Ulrik experimented with different ratios to optimize the time it would take to launch one piece of candy, reset the spoon, and send the next piece of candy aloft.

The next step was to integrate a mechanism that would reload the spoon with the next piece of candy. Ulrik sketched some designs and built another small prototype of the reloading mechanism. As he constructed it, he kept fully-built copies of each version of each of the parts of the catapult as references to help him when trying to improve the various parts.

note: *Keeping your prototypes is a great way to build truly great models. If you don't have enough LEGO elements to keep full copies of each version of each part, consider drawing up your results on paper before taking a model apart.*

The final major step was to synchronize the launching and reloading mechanisms so they would work fluidly and continuously. When trying to integrate the launching and reloading mechanisms, Ulrik created a few more versions of each and was able to drive the entire assembly with only one motor and a minimum number of gears.

LEGO RULES BROKEN

As described in the PPL project, LEGO does not approve of designs that incorporate non-LEGO pieces or that require modifications to any of the components. This means that the simple plastic spoon in this model would never have worked at LEGO; not only is it a foreign object, but you also have to modify it to make it function properly in the CCC.

NON-LEGO PARTS USED

The first non-LEGO part is the spoon. But who has not used the spoon flipping principle either in school or at the dinner table? In a similar manner, the force applied to the plastic spoon (and, consequently, the distance the candy will be flung) can be adjusted using the worm gear in the front of the model.

note: *Performance may vary depending on the plastic spoon's make and model. Check with the manufacturer first or read your spoon's user manual.*

The second non-LEGO component is a piece of thick paper or cardboard that will serve as a magazine to hold the candy. You can modify this paper magazine to hold as many pieces of candy as you want!

Have you ever wanted a piece of candy but were too lazy to get out of your favorite chair and go get one? Well, until now you had only a few choices: hire a butler, have some kids (and wait until they can walk), or just stop being so darn lazy.

Now you have another choice. With our Candy Coated Catapult (CCC), you can magically loft candy across the room without moving an inch! This model makes round candy airborne and then automatically reloads the next piece. It uses the well-known and time-tested "spoon-flip principle"—annoying to some junior high students, loved by others.

HOW IT WORKS

1. The motor uses a 15:1 gearing system to turn a lift arm that pushes the plastic spoon down until it clicks into launch ready mode.

2. The automatic reload mechanism loads a piece of candy by sliding it through two doors in front of the magazine. The piece falls into the spoon.

3. The motor forces the plastic spoon to come up, flipping it with great force and sending the piece of candy flying!

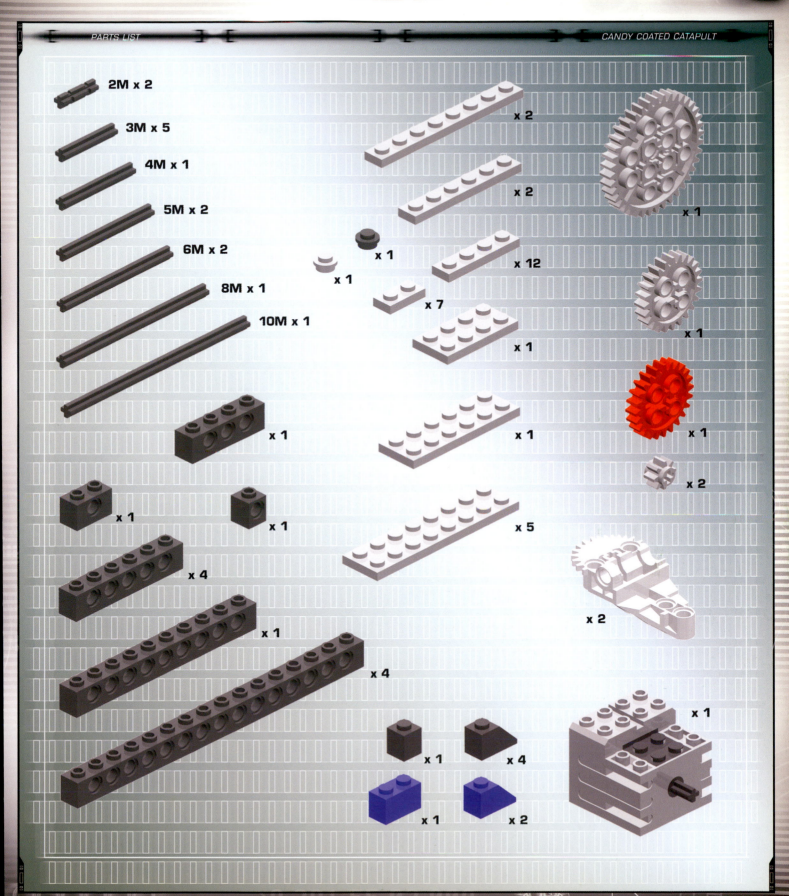

2M x 2

3M x 5

4M x 1

5M x 2

6M x 2

8M x 1

10M x 1

x 2

x 2

x 1

x 1

x 12

x 7

x 1

x 1

x 1

x 1

x 1

x 1

x 5

x 1

x 2

x 4

x 1

x 2

x 4

x 1

x 1

x 4

x 1

x 4

x 2

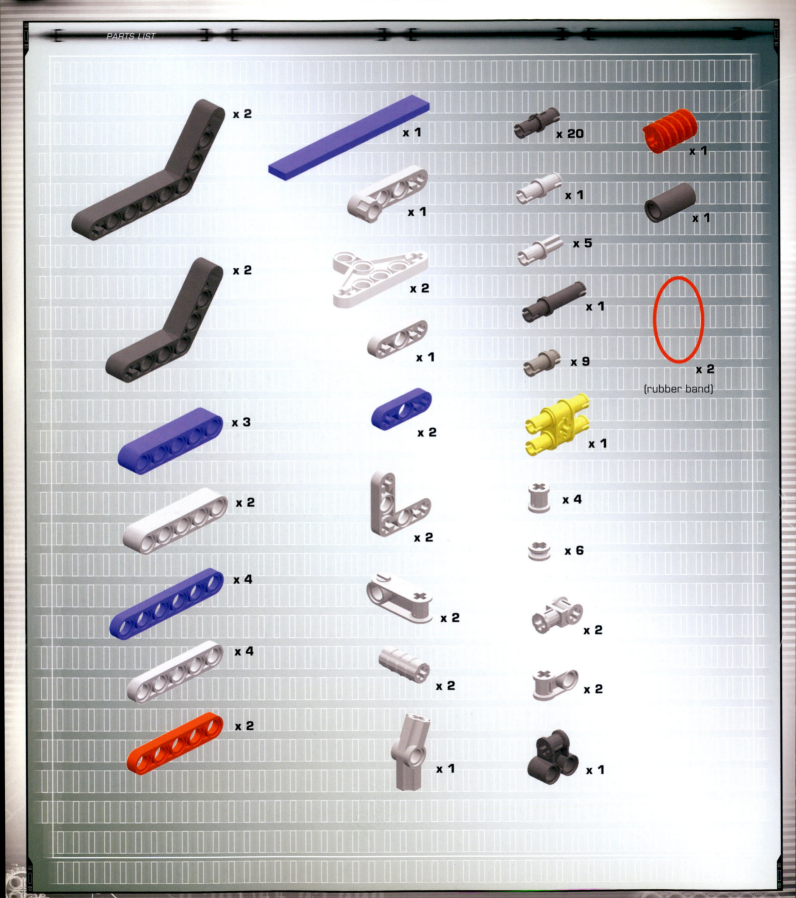

x 2

x 1

x 1

x 20

x 1

x 2

x 1

x 5

x 2

x 1

x 1

x 3

x 1

x 9

x 2

(rubber band)

x 2

x 2

x 1

x 4

x 4

x 2

x 6

x 4

x 2

x 2

x 2

x 2

x 2

x 1

x 1

x 1

10M

3M

x 1   x 1   x 1   x 2

1. Gather all the pieces shown here to build this spoon assembly.

2. You need to modify the spoon by cutting a ridge where the LEGO crossaxel can fit and hold the spoon in place.

3. Make your cut so that the distance between the cut and the end of the spoon match these guidelines.

   The head of the plastic spoon can not exceed 1 1/4" (32 mm) in width.

4. Make sure the spoon sits securely between the 2 triangles and proceed with the building instruction on the following pages.

5.3"–5.7" [13.5–14.5cm]

10   3

B8HG562K7625ZZF57628U52618F62K8
2.342.7483.98416.88.958.3847.27843

B8HG87H543267857628U52618F62K8
9.342.7483.87516.88.958.3847.27843

001

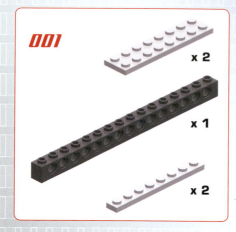

x 2

x 1

x 2

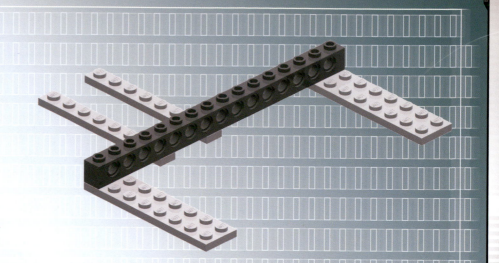

002

x 4

x 1

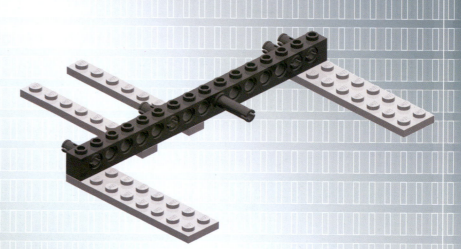

003

x 1

x 1

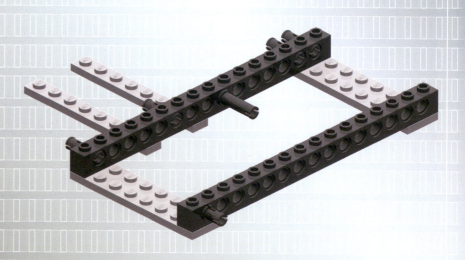

004

x 2

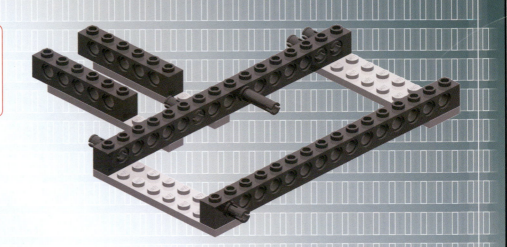

005

x 2

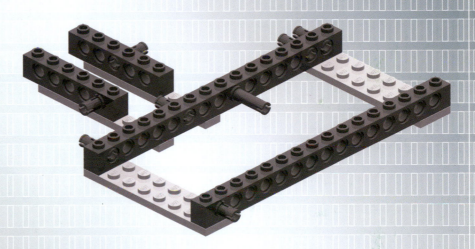

006
 x 1
 x 1   x 5

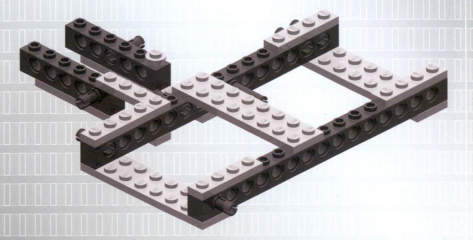

007

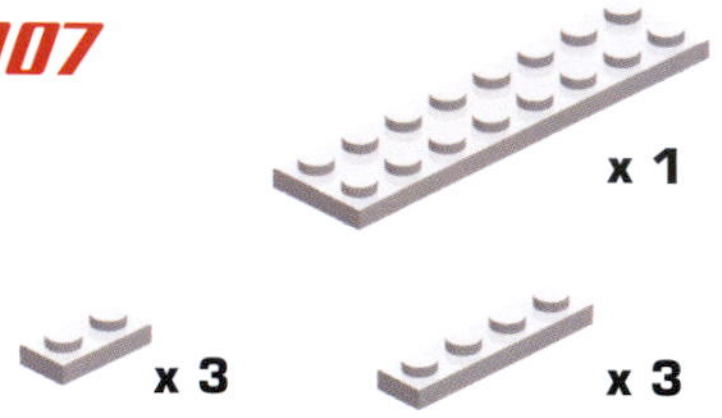

x 1

x 3   x 3

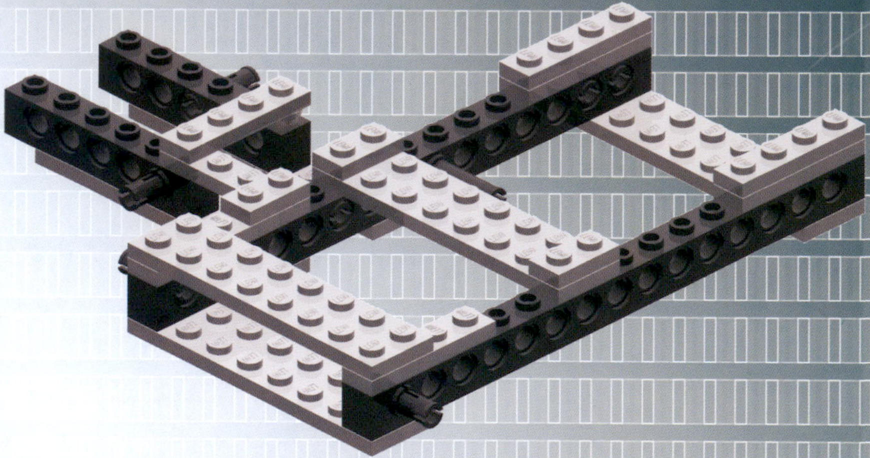

008

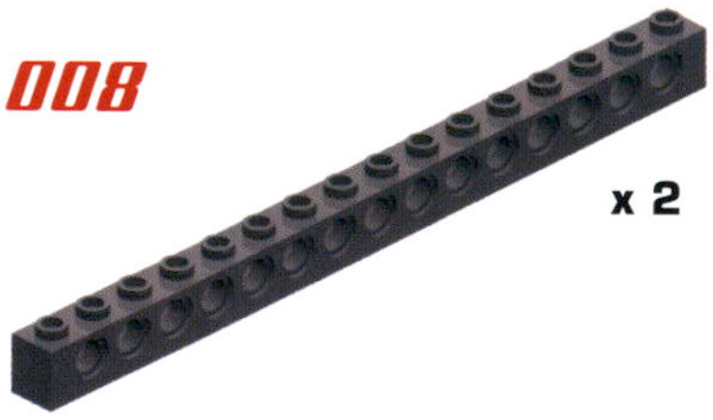

x 2

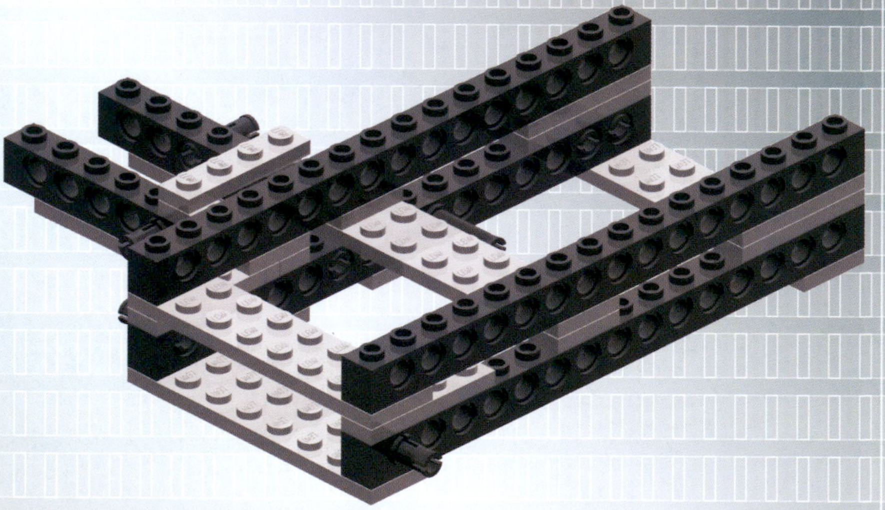

009

x 2

x 5   x 1

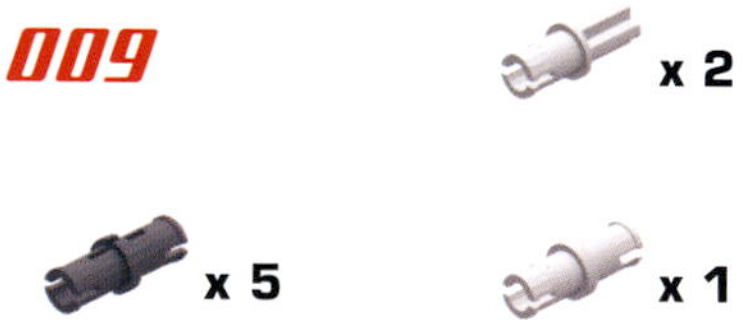

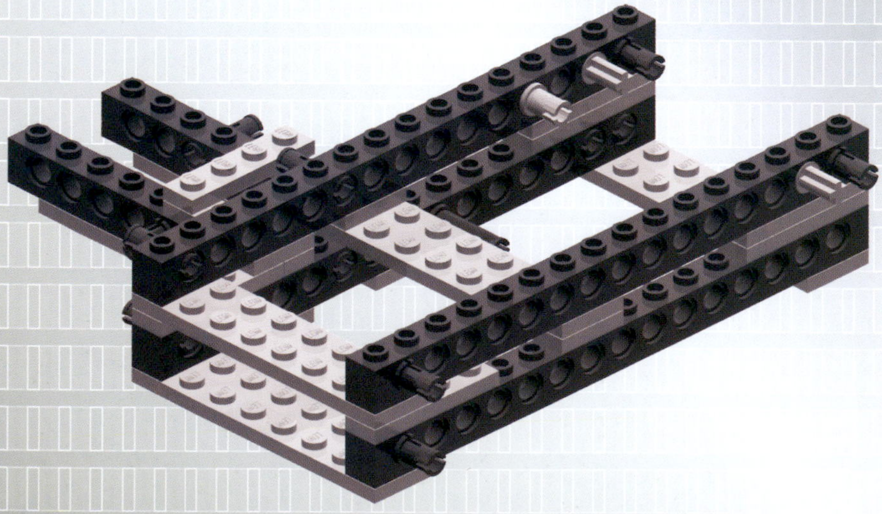

010

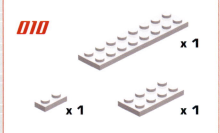

x 1

x 1   x 1

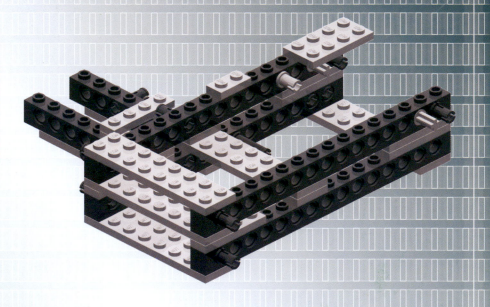

011

x 3

x 1

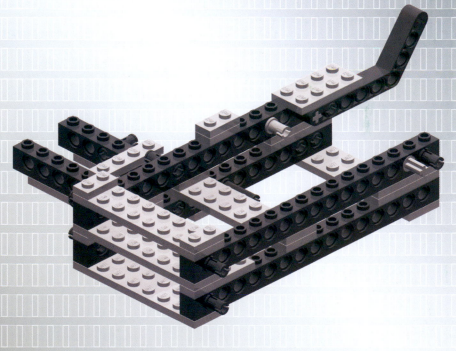

BUILDING STEPS

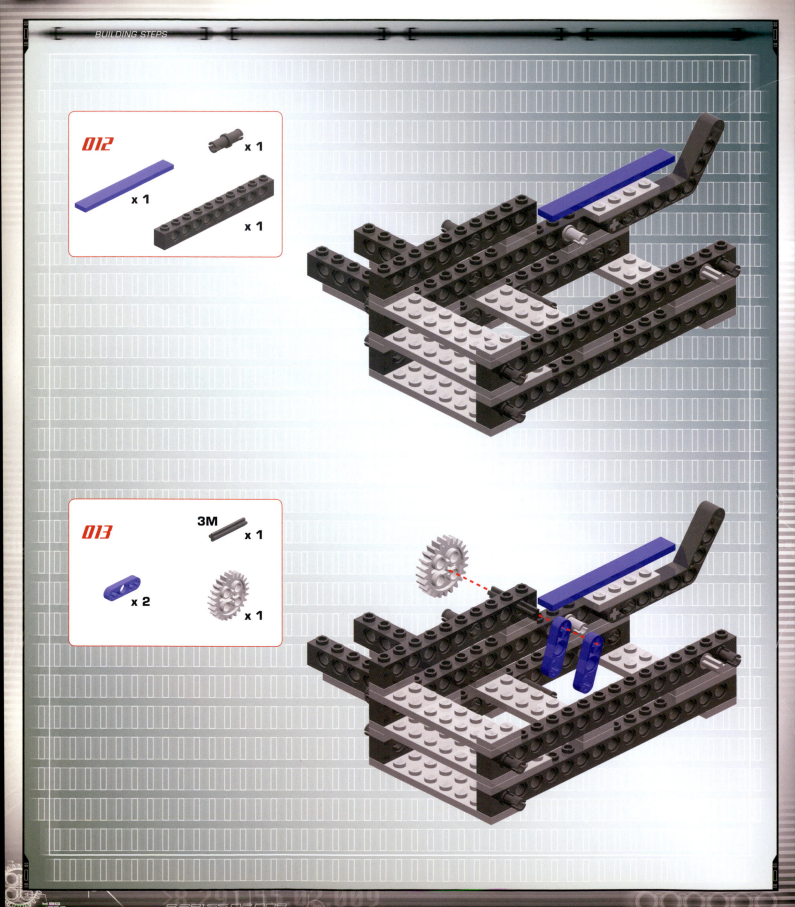

012

x 1

x 1

013

3M

x 1

x 2

x 1

014

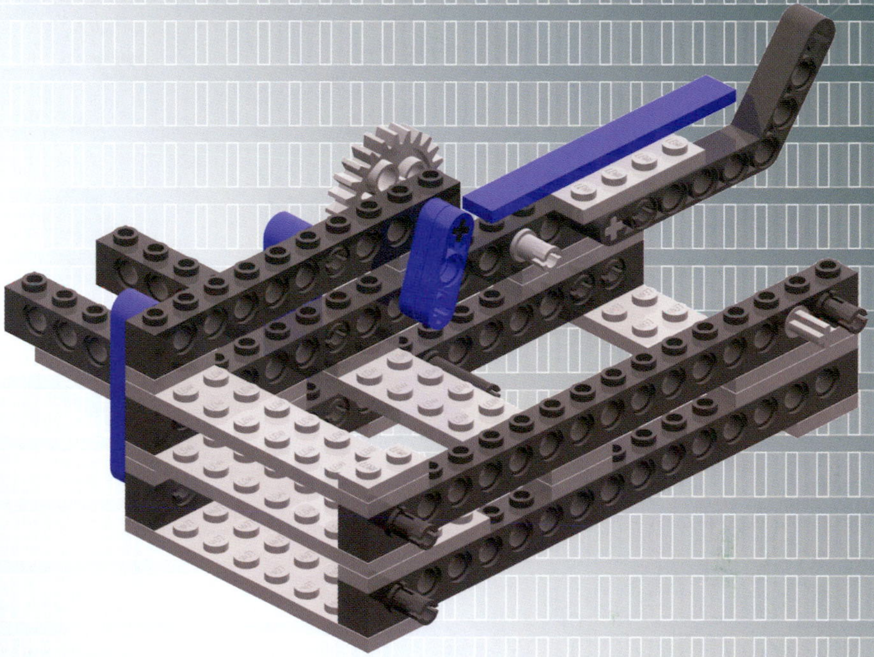

015

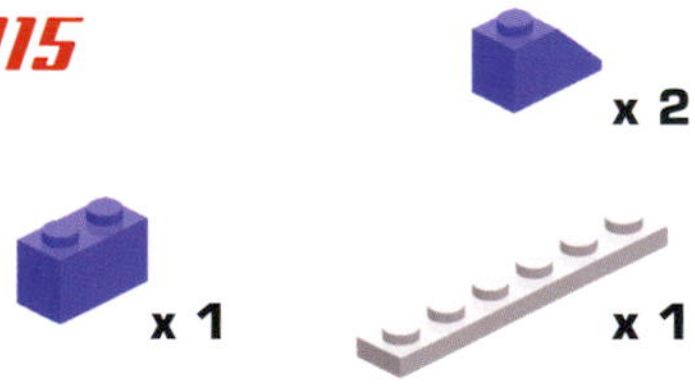

x 2

x 1

x 1

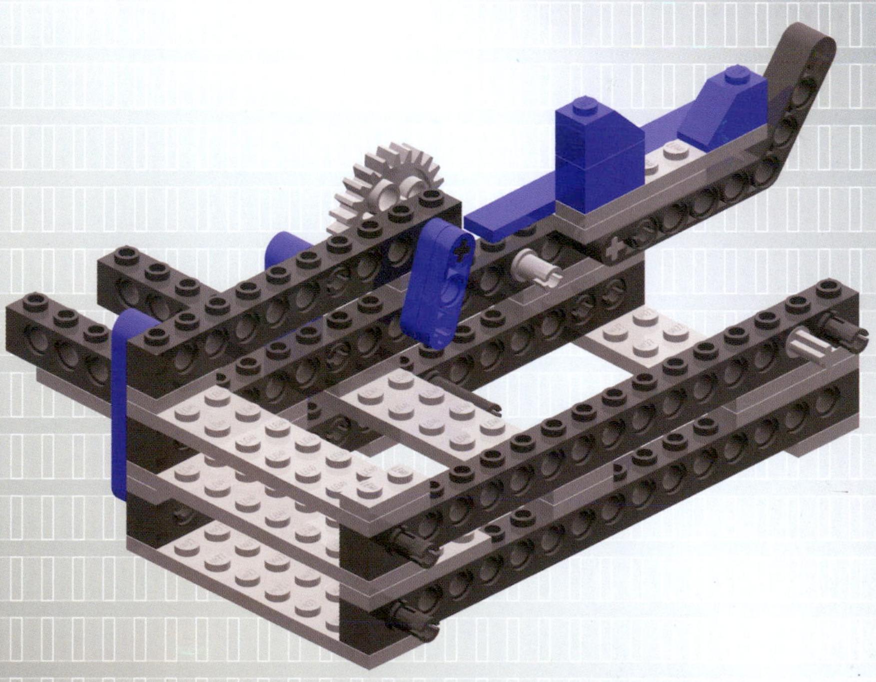

016

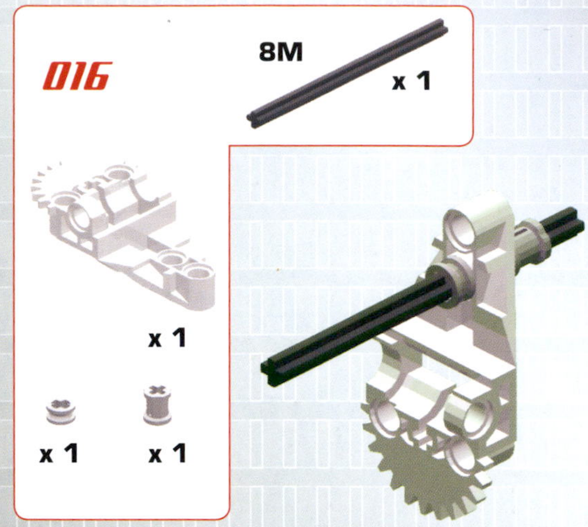

8M
x 1

x 1

x 1   x 1

017

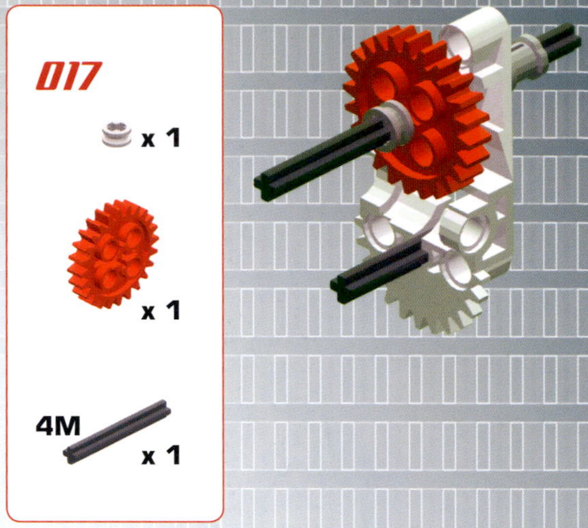

x 1

x 1

4M
x 1

018

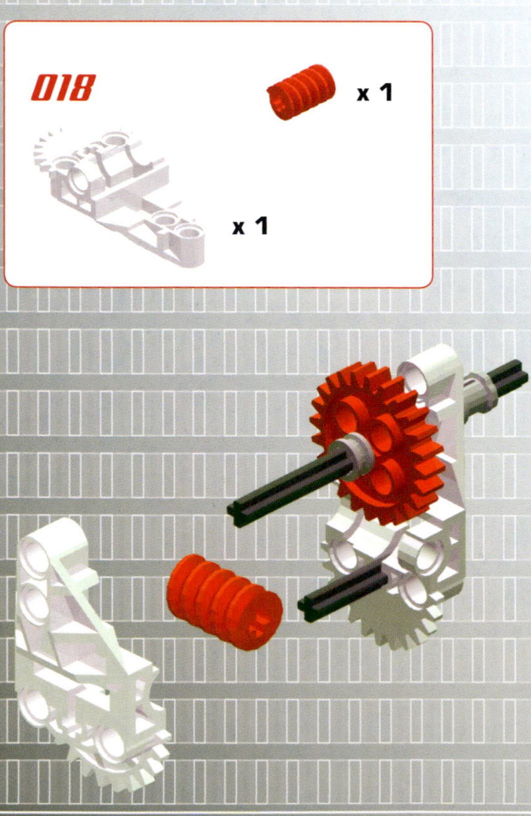

x 1

x 1

019

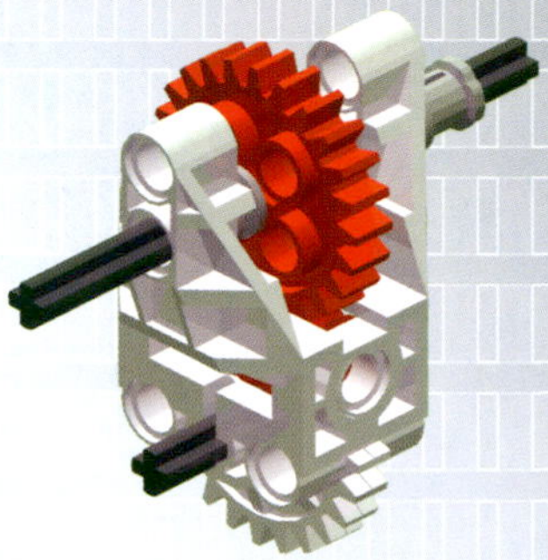

020 x 1 x 1

5M x 1

021 x 1

x 1

x 1

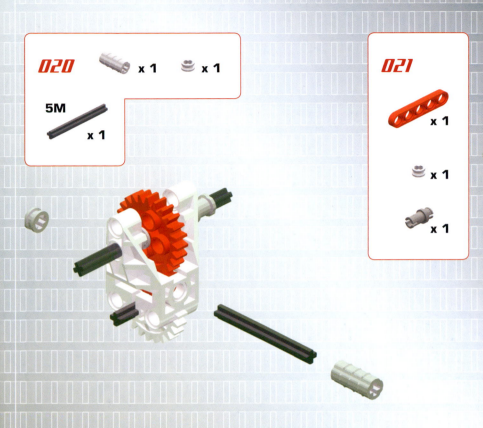

022 x 1

x 1

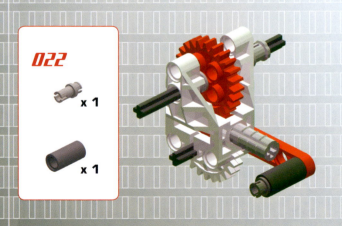

023 x 1

x 1 x 1

x 1

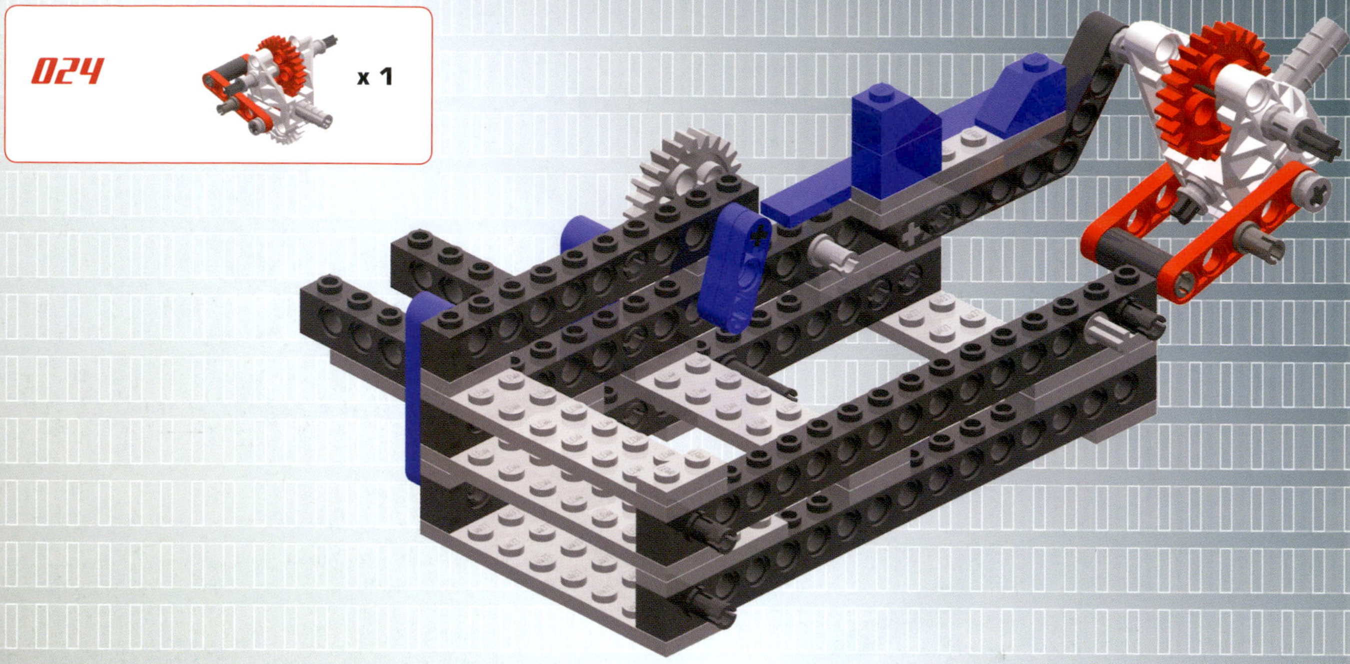

024 x 1

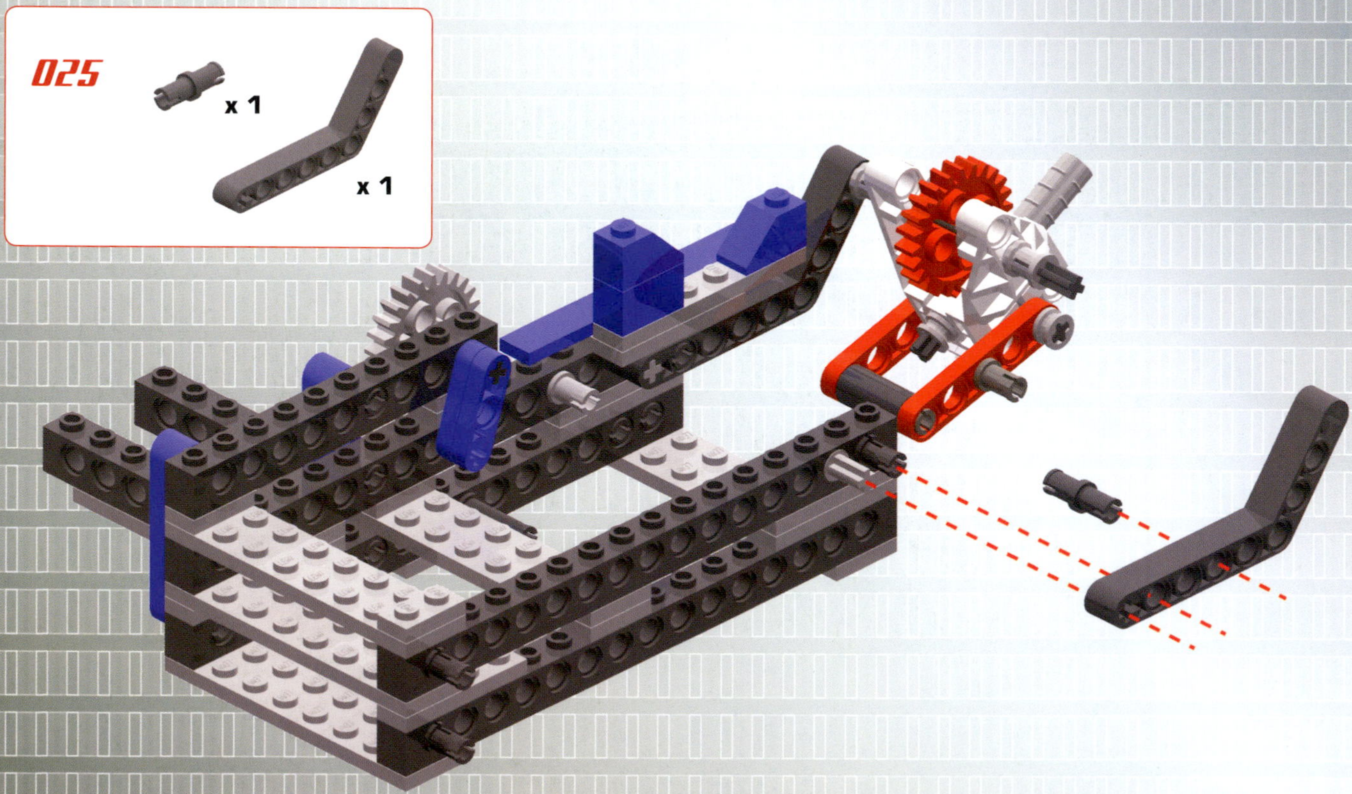

025 x 1 x 1

026

027

Use the assembly that you created from the Tip instructions at the beginning of this project.

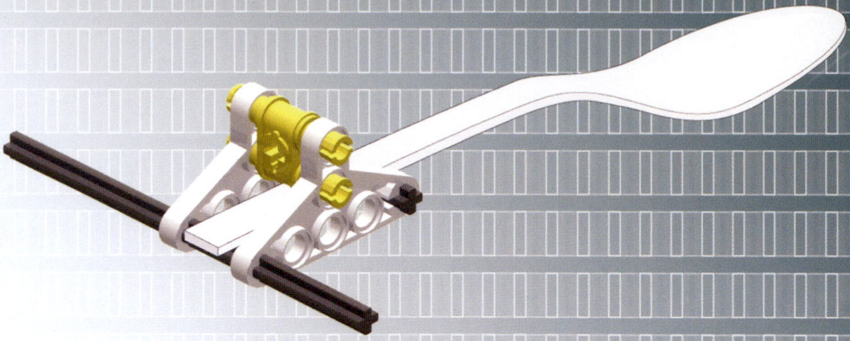

028

x 1

x 1

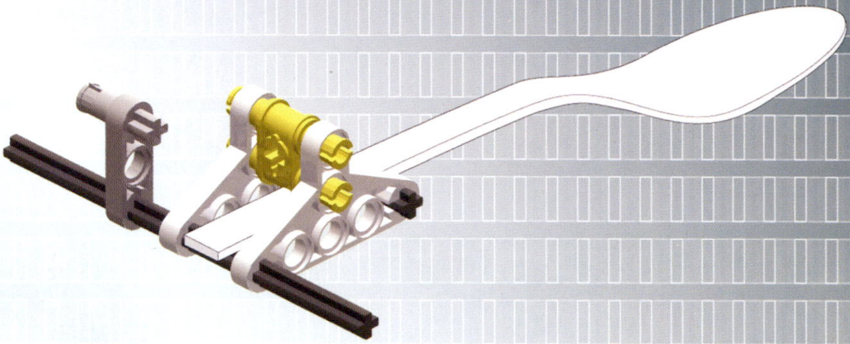

029

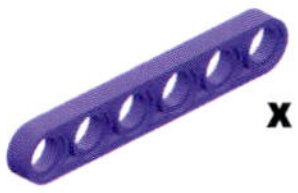

x 2

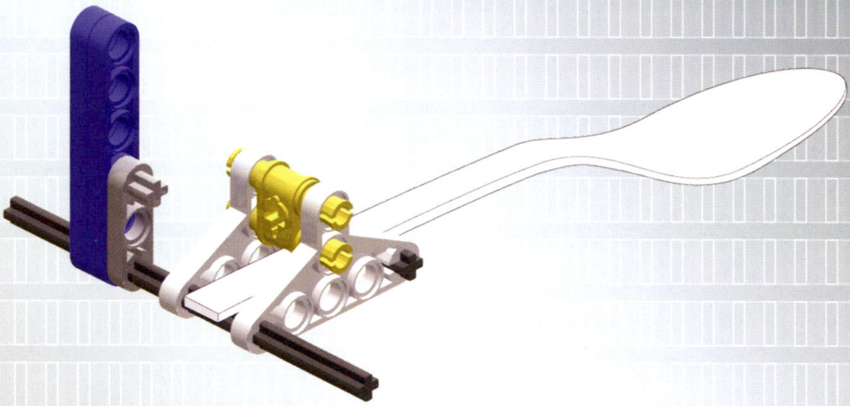

030

x 1

x 1

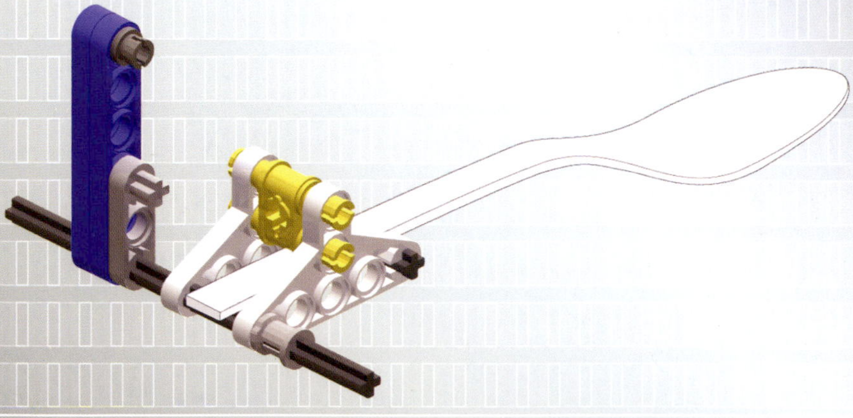

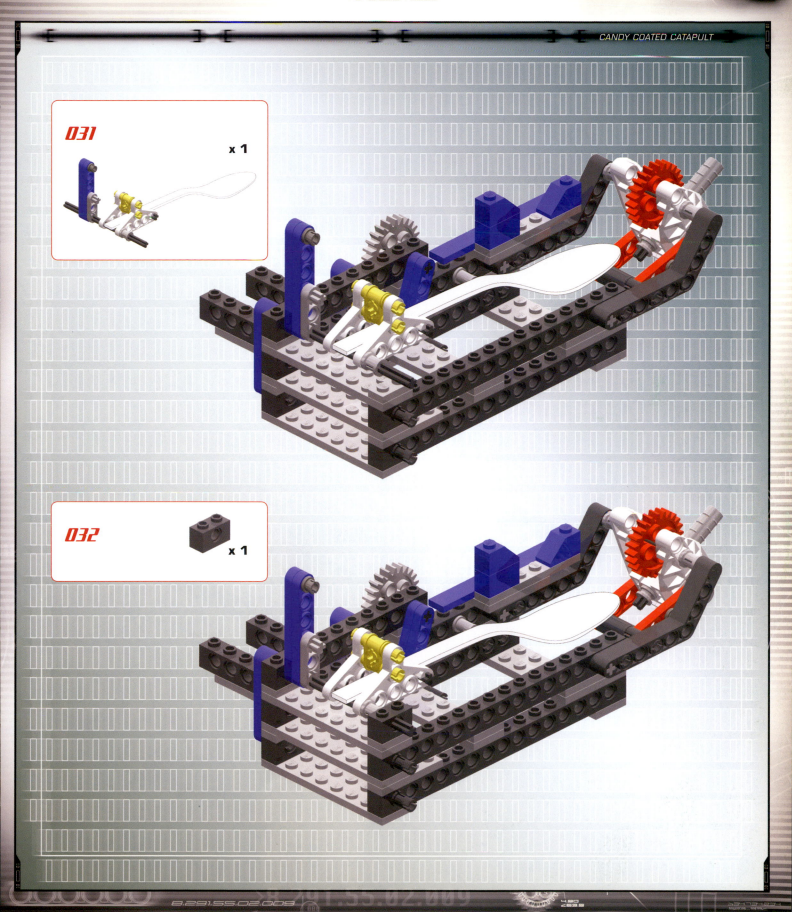

031   x 1

032   x 1

033

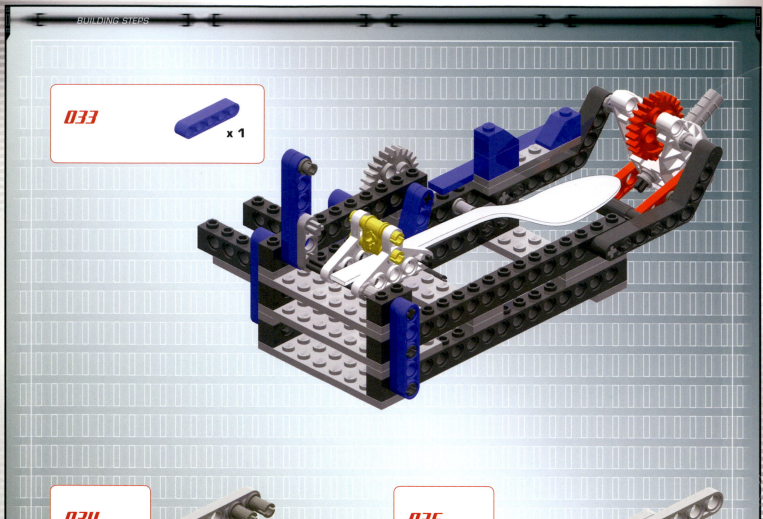

x 1

034

x 1

x 4

035

x 2

036

x 1

037

2M 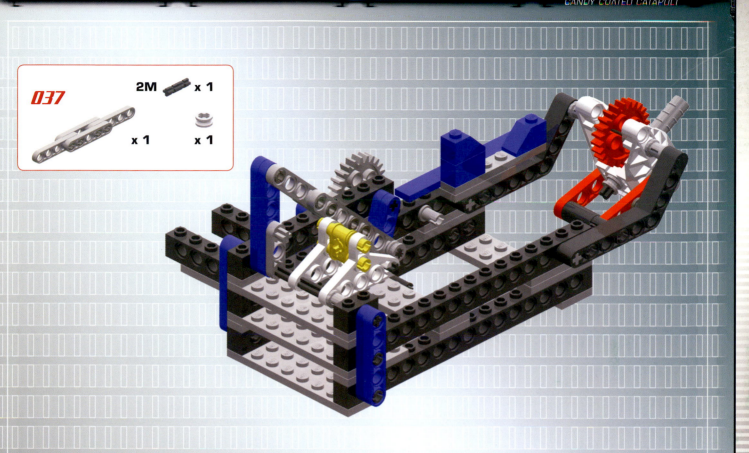 x 1

x 1   x 1

038

x 1   5M   x 1

x 1

x 1

039

x 1

3M   x 1

040

x 2

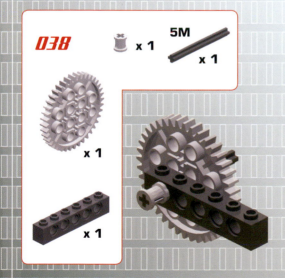

041

x 1

042

x 1

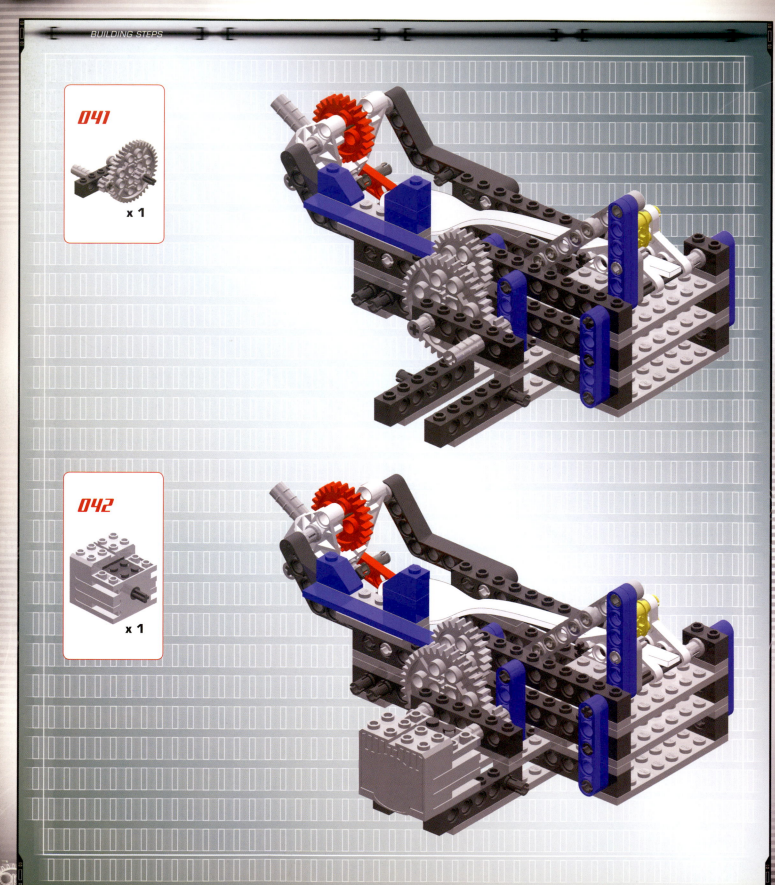

043

x 2

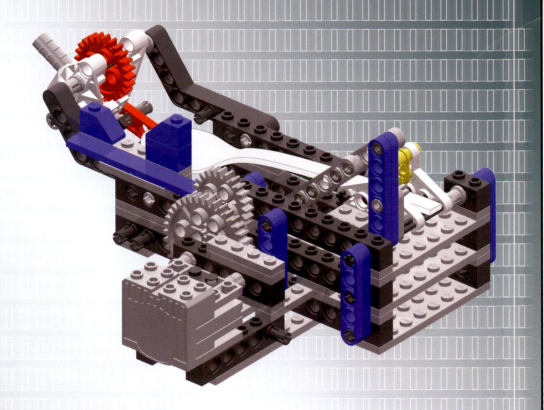

044

x 1

x 1

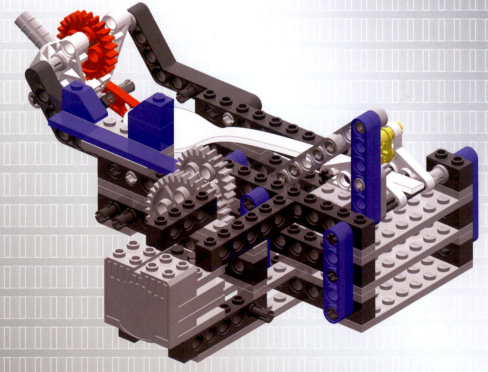

BUILDING STEPS

045

x 1

x 2

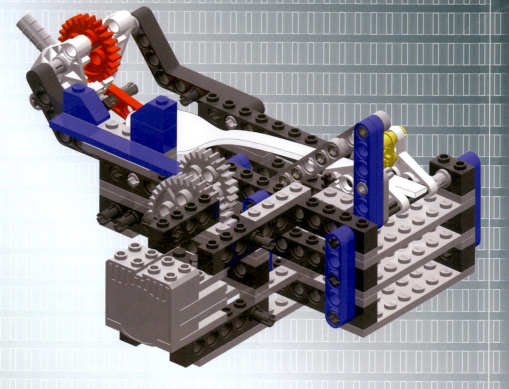

046

x 2

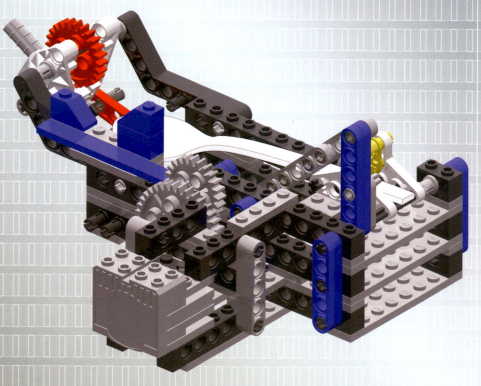

047

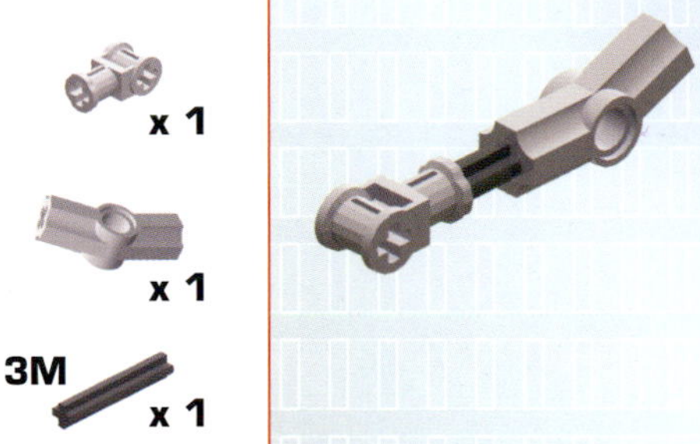

x 1

x 1

3M x 1

048

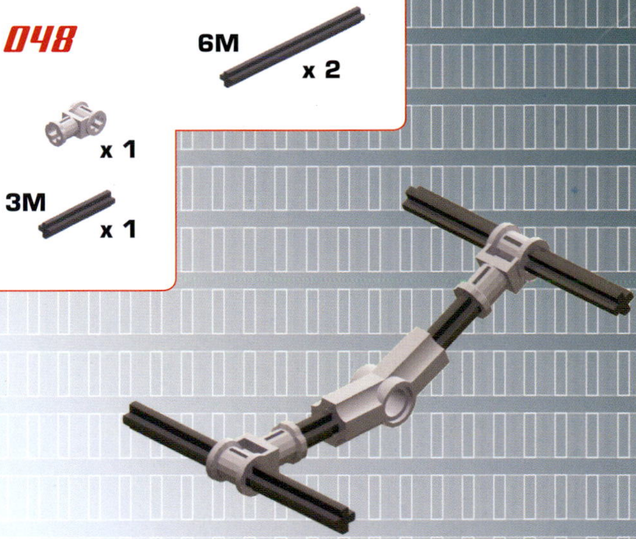

6M x 2

x 1

3M x 1

049

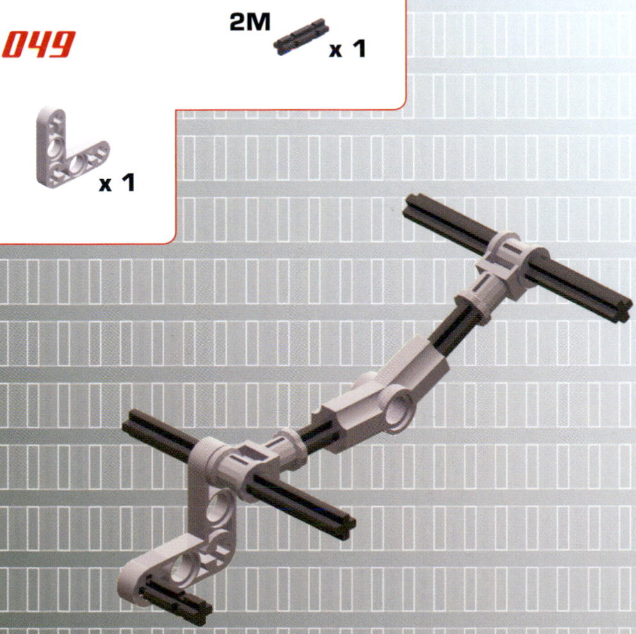

2M x 1

x 1

050

x 1

x 1

BUILDING STEPS

051 x 2 x 2

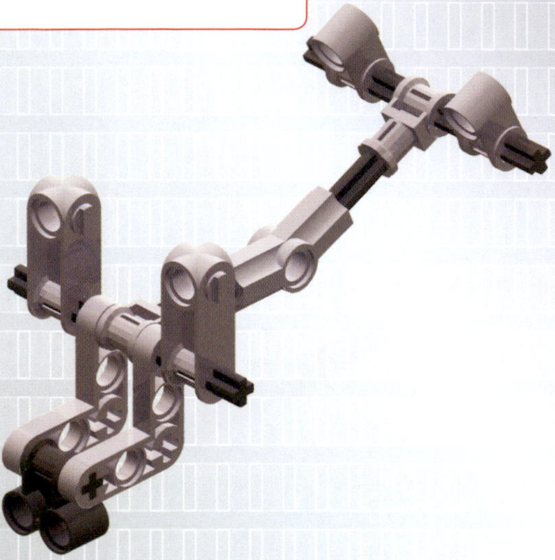

052 x 4

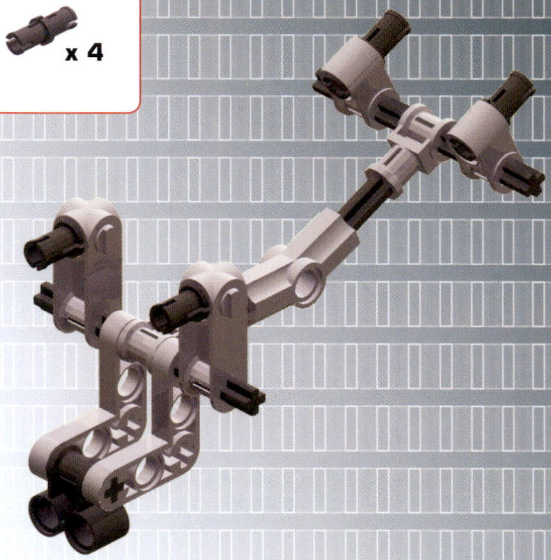

053 x 2

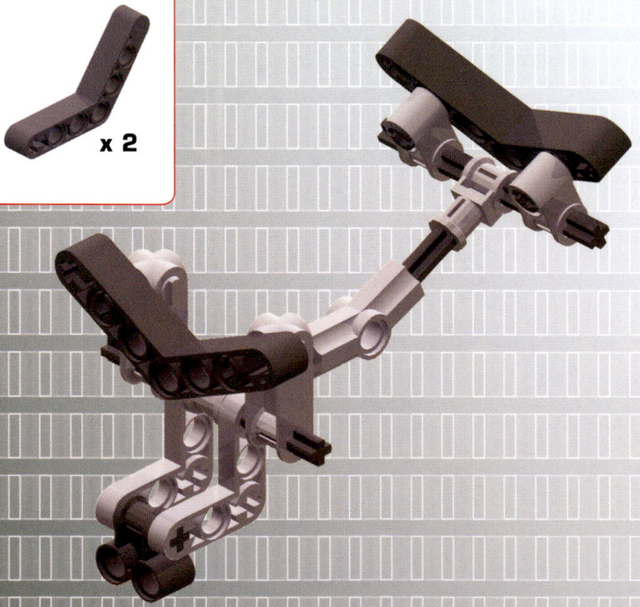

054

Use a piece of paper to create the Candy Conveyor belt.

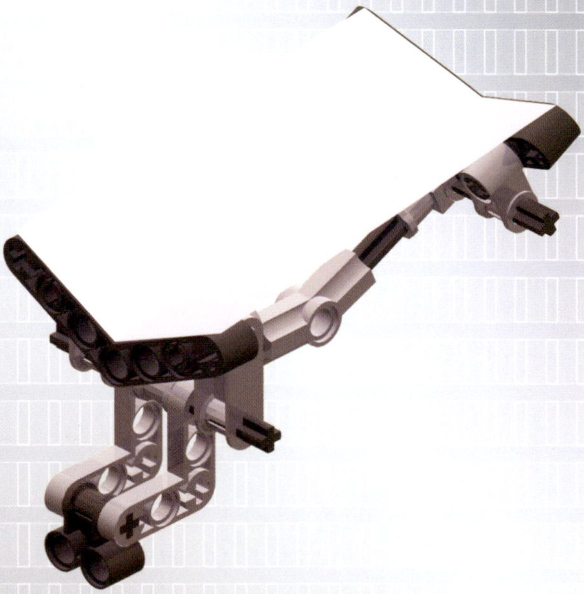

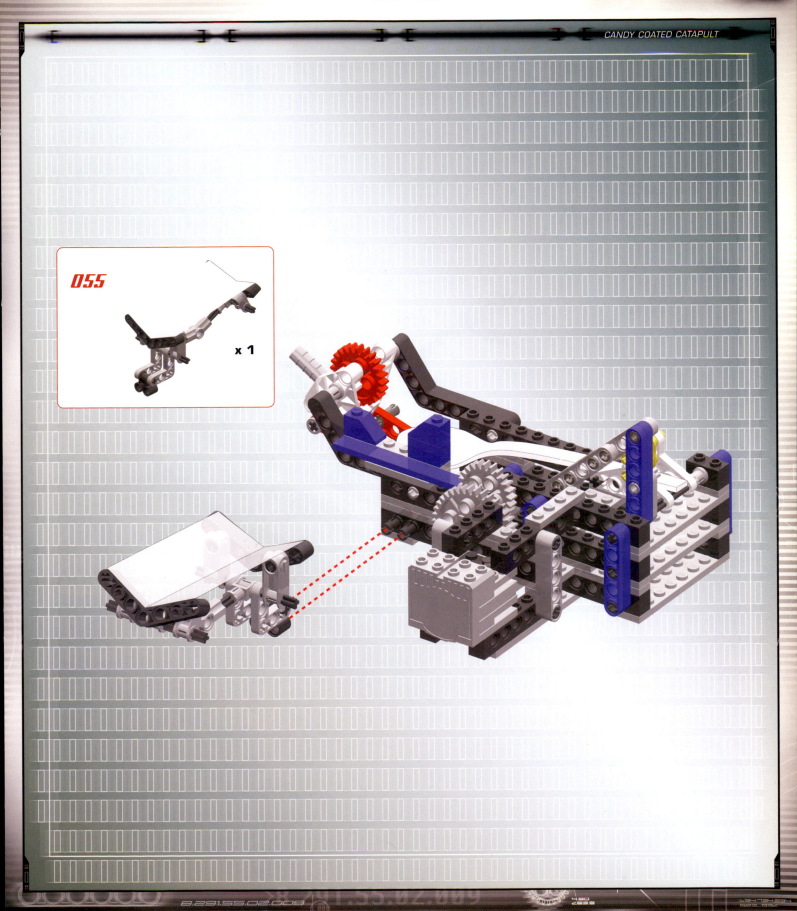

055

x 1

056

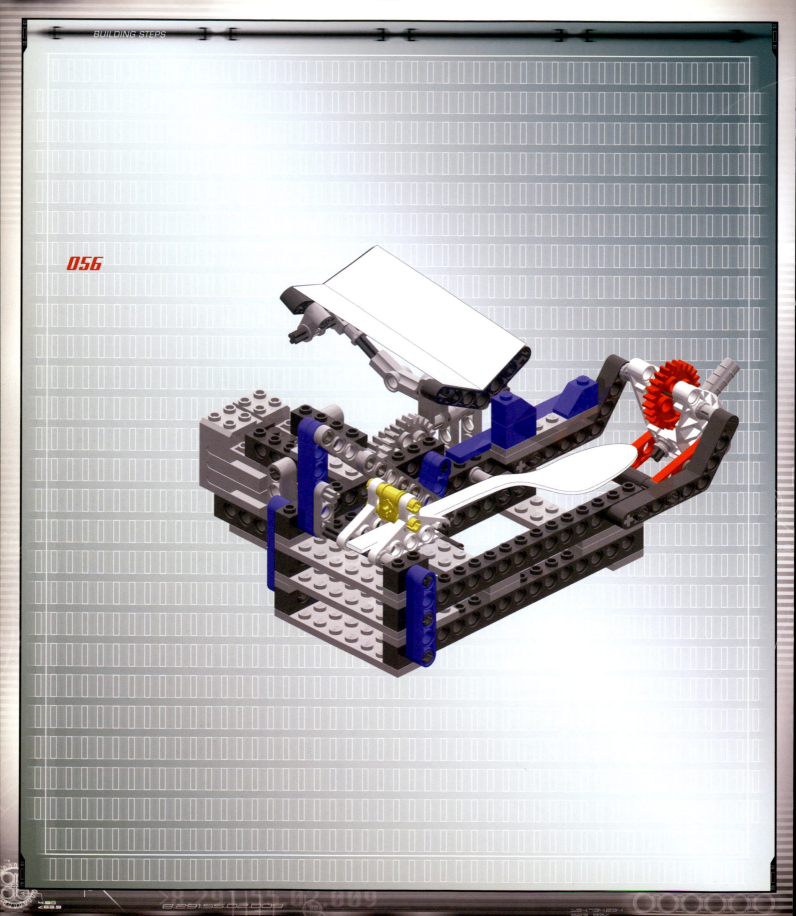

057

 x 1

 x 1

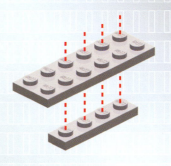

058

 x 1

 x 2

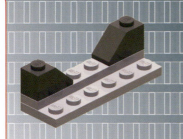

059

 x 1

 x 1

060

 x 1

 x 1

 x 1

061

 x 1

 x 1

062

 x 1

 x 2

063

x 1

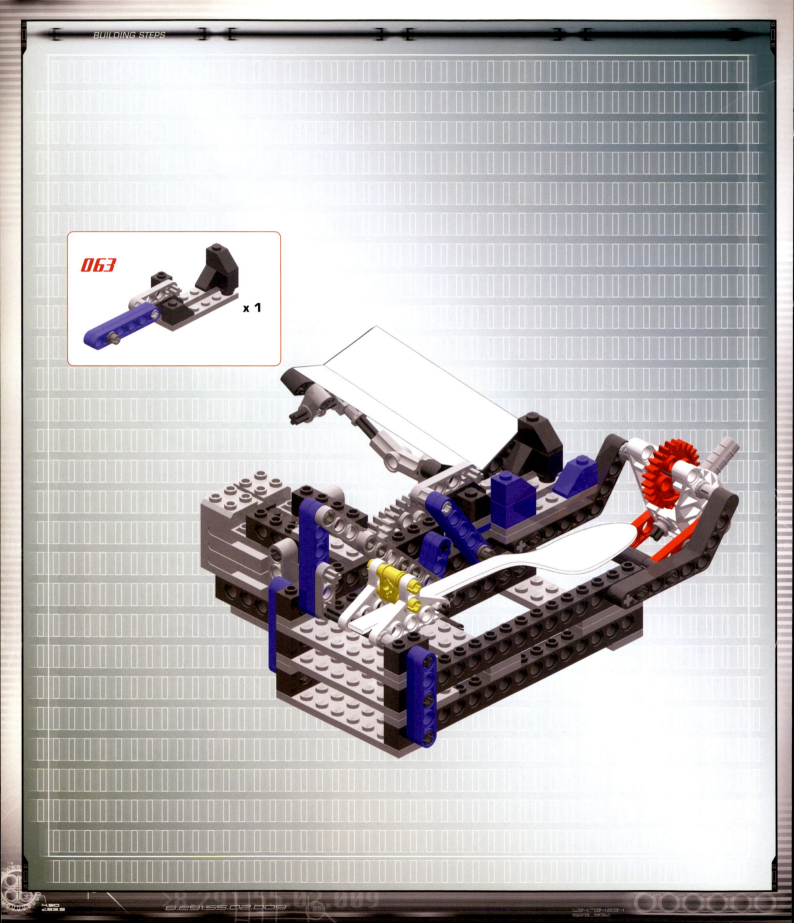

064

x 2

(rubber band)

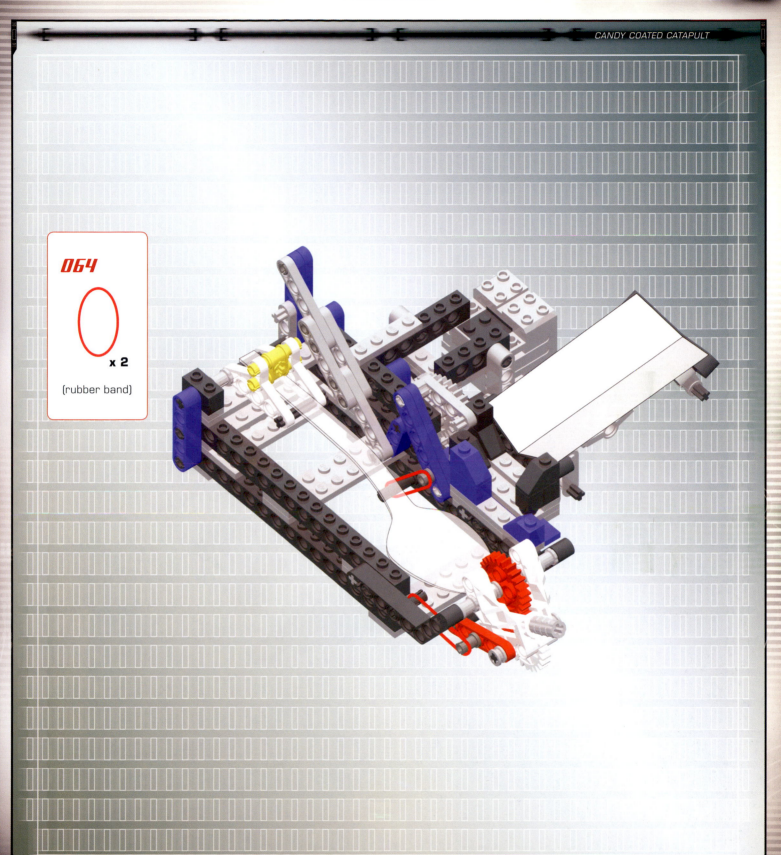

065

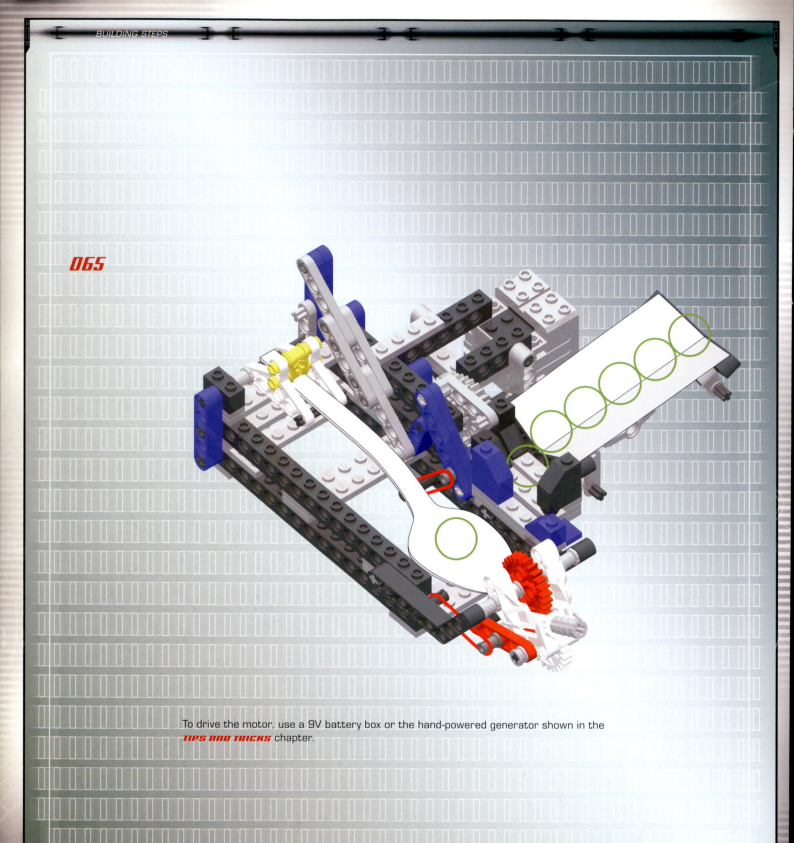

To drive the motor, use a 9V battery box or the hand-powered generator shown in the *TIPS AND TRICKS* chapter.

PROJECT 3:
PING-PONG CANNON (PPC)

THE INSPIRATION

You can build a replica or prototype of any mechanical contraption with LEGO bricks. And with all of the new LEGO elements released every year, it keeps getting easier to design models that look almost like the real thing.

Take the PPC, for example, which uses only three "normal" beams with studs. While we didn't set out to build this model with as few studded beams as possible, stud-free pieces are the way to go if one of your goals is to build a real-looking contraption.

note: *As with all of the building instructions in this book, if you don't have one of the pieces shown, just use what you have. For example, you could replace most of the PPC's stud-free beams with studded ones without compromising the model's functionality.*

THE DESIGN

In order to hold the ping-pong ball "ammunition," we added a magazine that allows the balls to fall down one by one and lock into position, ready for launch. When designing this magazine, we began by creating two bars on which the balls could roll. Next, we added side walls so the balls would not fall out during the model's operation. Finally, we added a cross axle to make sure the balls would stay put once they were in the launch position. (You should adjust the length of this cross axle to optimize performance of your model.)

One design challenge was getting the unit to function in a circular way so that it would fire all of the balls in the magazine in one continuous motion. It's particularly handy to be able to fire all of the balls at once, especially if you choose to hook the cannon up as a burglar alarm or if you just want to watch five ping-pong balls bouncing all over your room at the same time.

The beam that strikes the ping-pong balls works more or less in the same way that a baseball pitching machine operates, except that a pitching machine uses two wheels to accelerate the balls smoothly and accurately. (Maybe we'll redesign the PPC to look more like a two-wheeled pitching machine for the second edition!)

LEGO RULES BROKEN

Ping-pong balls are considered relatively safe, and have a pretty low ranking on LEGO's hazardous objects list. Their smooth surface, large size, and low weight limit how much damage they can do to a person. There are companies that sell toy ping-pong ball shooters rated for kids as young as four years old; however, LEGO isn't one of those companies.

The first LEGO rule broken with this model is actually the ping-pong ball itself. If launched with enough speed, a ping-pong ball could tear the plastic wrap in the test used to assess eye safety risks. LEGO would probably opt to use a foam ball instead, since a foam ball has a nice soft surface, is lighter in weight, and hits with less force than a ping-pong ball. Unfortunately, foam balls aren't nearly as much fun as ping-pong balls because they don't fly as far when launched, they definitely don't bounce around as much, and they don't make as much noise!

The second problem, which you'll recall from the introduction, is that someone could put a foreign, non-LEGO object (like a stone or some sort of popper) in place of the ping-pong ball. This is clearly a LEGO no-no.

NON-LEGO PARTS USED

Ping-pong balls are the only non-LEGO part you need here. Because ping-pong balls come in a standard size, you should be able to find some that fit in the PPC's loading chamber at any sporting goods store.

For greater optimization of your PPC, experiment with the size and strength of the model's rubber bands. Look for a rubber band that will apply maximum force to the launch beam without preventing the motor from rotating.

PING-PONG CANNON

Bounce ping-pong balls around your room until your head spins! This invention will hold five ping-pong balls and launch them at you from up to 10 feet away. That's far enough to use the Ping-Pong Cannon (PPC) as a table tennis buddy, a personal room protector, or even a baseball trainer.

Experiment by adding more rubber bands and more power to the motor to see how far you can extend your PPC's range. As a rule, adding more power almost always raises the coolness factor of any LEGO invention.

NOTE: *For a head start, check out the Tips and Tricks chapter to see how to get 18V out of two 9V LEGO battery packs.*

HOW IT WORKS

1. The rack holds up to five ping-pong balls; the bottom ball is in the launching position.

2. A hinged arm rotates around the base of the stack. The hinge allows the outer beam of the arm to bend just like your elbow allows your forearm to bend. The rubber bands work like muscles—they flex to keep the two beams of the arm extended straight out.

3. As the arm approaches the bottom ping-pong ball, its path is blocked by a cross axle that is locked in place.

4. As the arm meets resistance against the cross axle, it bends at its hinge and the rubber bands stretch.

5. Because the arm is offset from the axis it rotates in, it bends so far that it eventually slips past the cross axle. As soon as the arm is free, the rubber bands pull the outer beam back to its original extended position, and with great and sudden force, the outer beam strikes the ping-pong ball and launches it into the air.

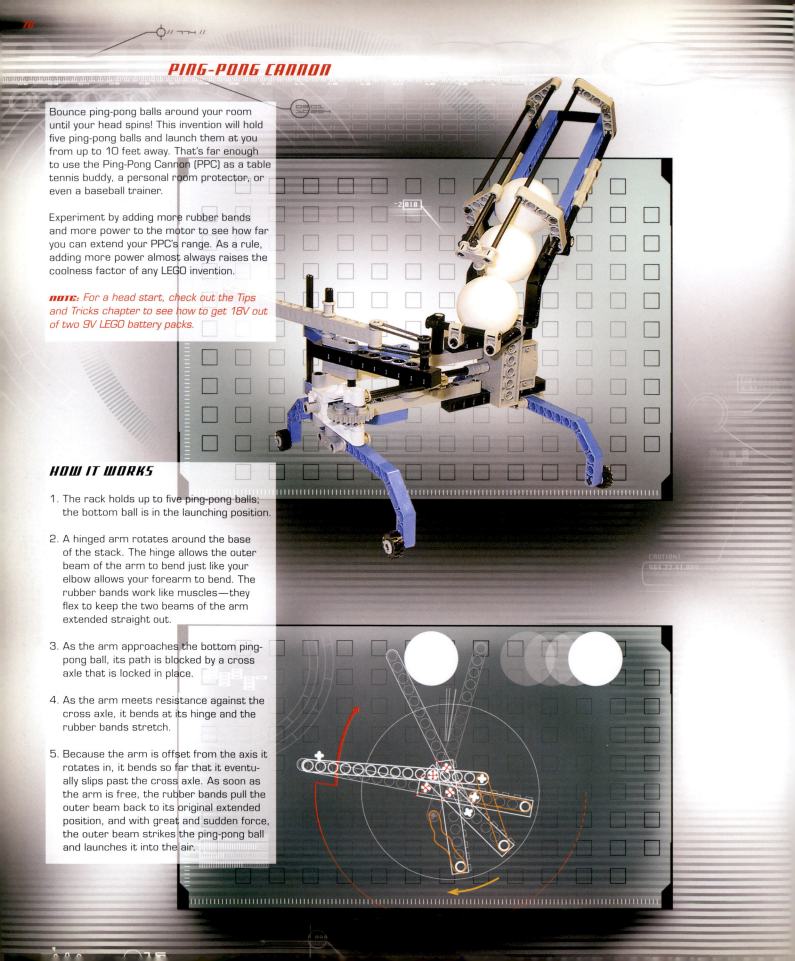

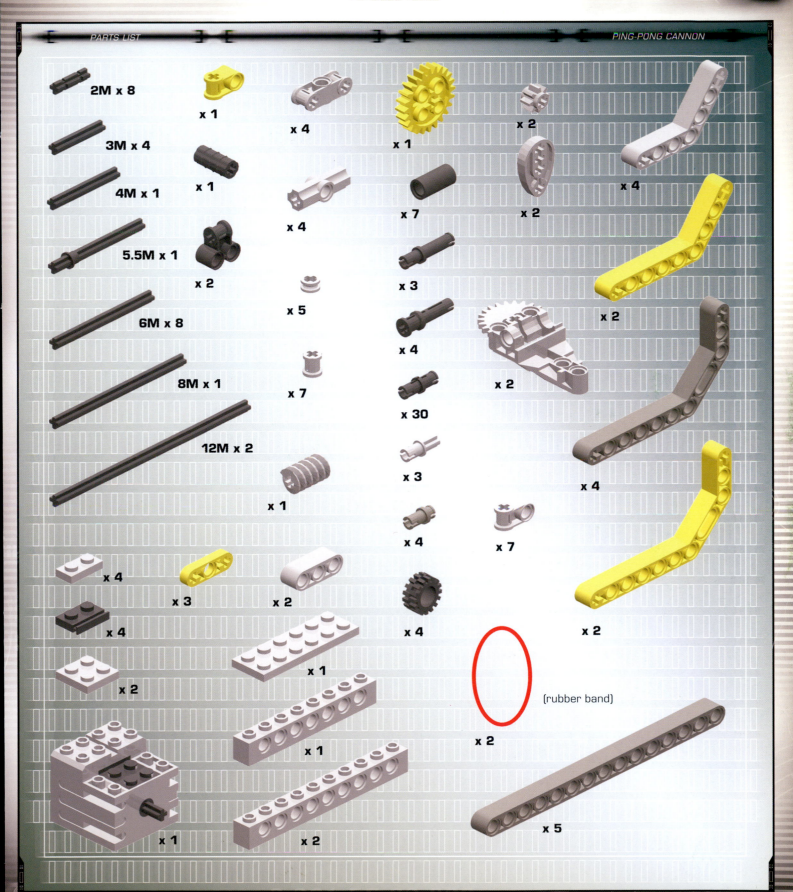

001

x 1

x 2

2M x 1

x 1

x 1

8M x 1

002

x 1

003

x 4

004

x 2

005

x 1

6M x 1

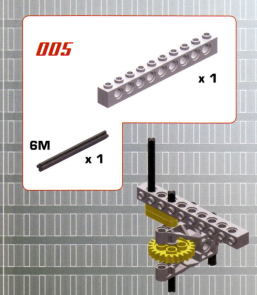

006

x 1

x 1

x 1

007

x 1

x 1

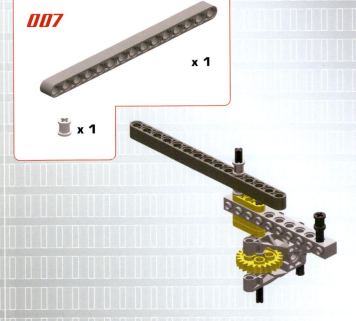

008

2M x 1

x 2

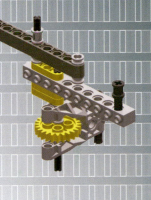

009

x 1

x 1

x 1

010

4M x 1

x 2

011

6M x 1

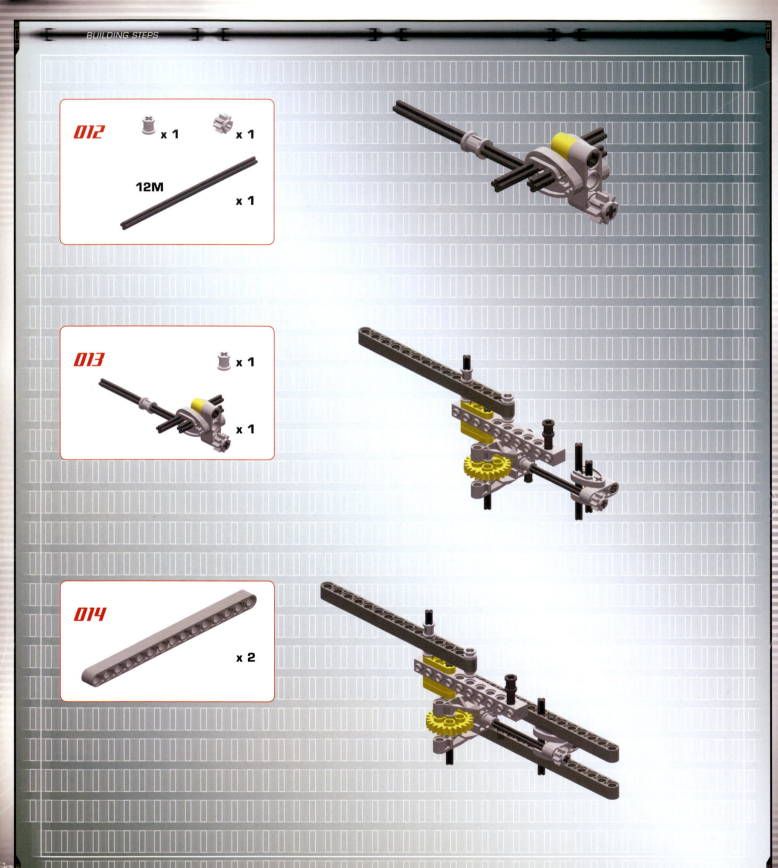

012

x 1

x 1

12M

x 1

013

x 1

x 1

014

x 2

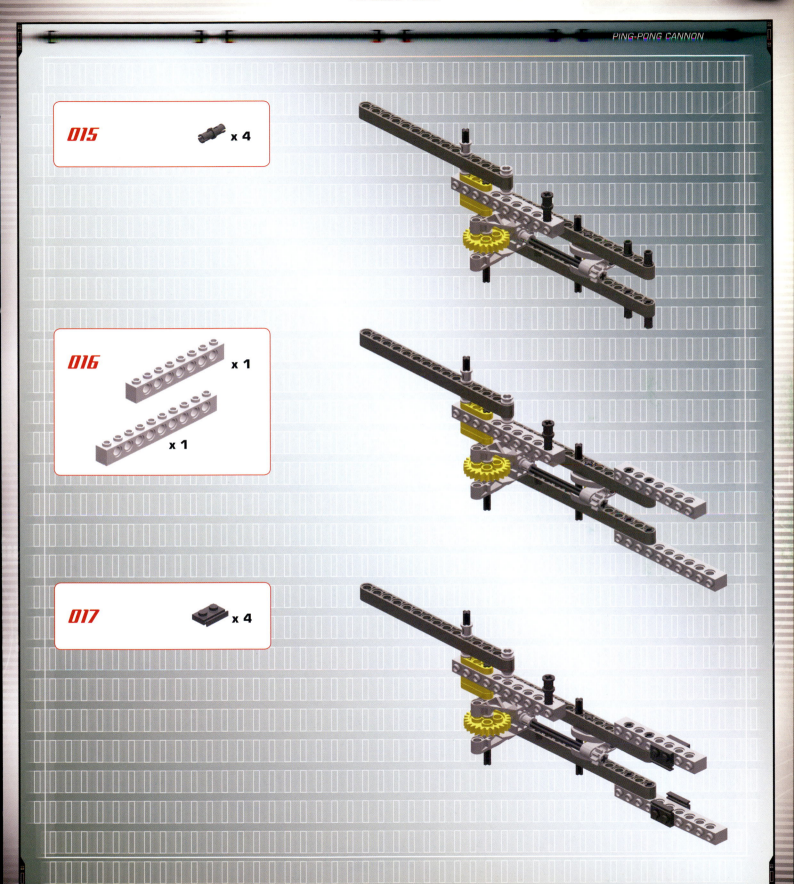

015 x 4

016 x 1
x 1

017 x 4

BUILDING STEPS

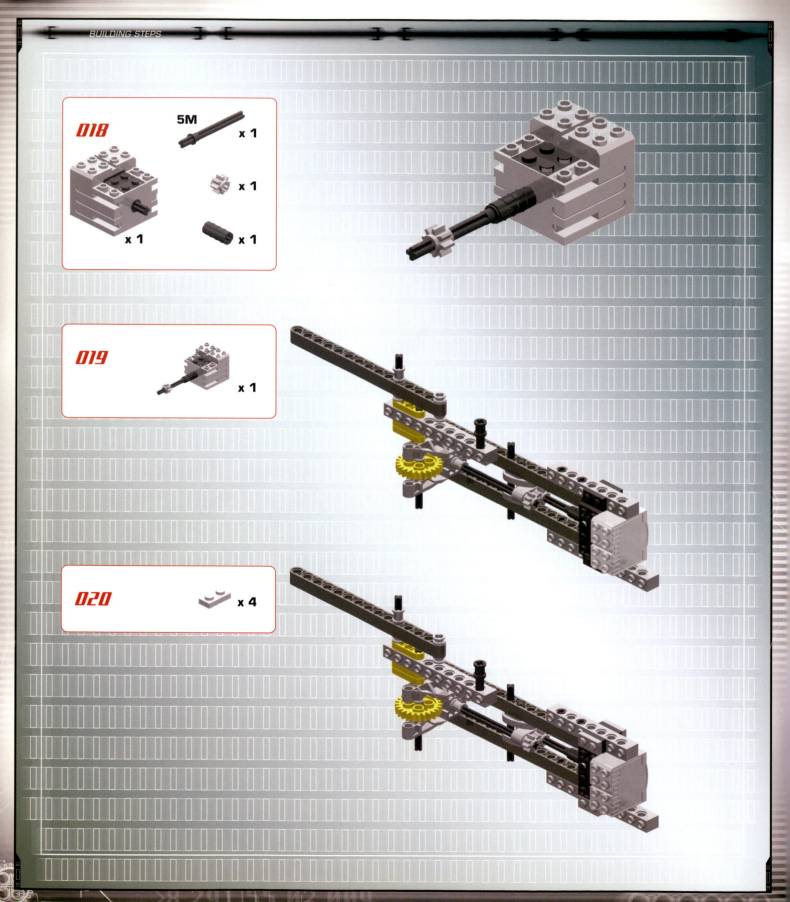

018

5M

x 1

x 1

x 1

x 1

019

x 1

020

x 4

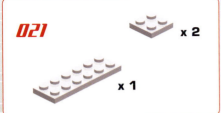

021

x 2

x 1

022

3M

x 2

x 2

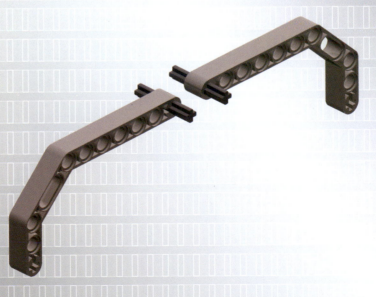

023 x 2

024 x 2

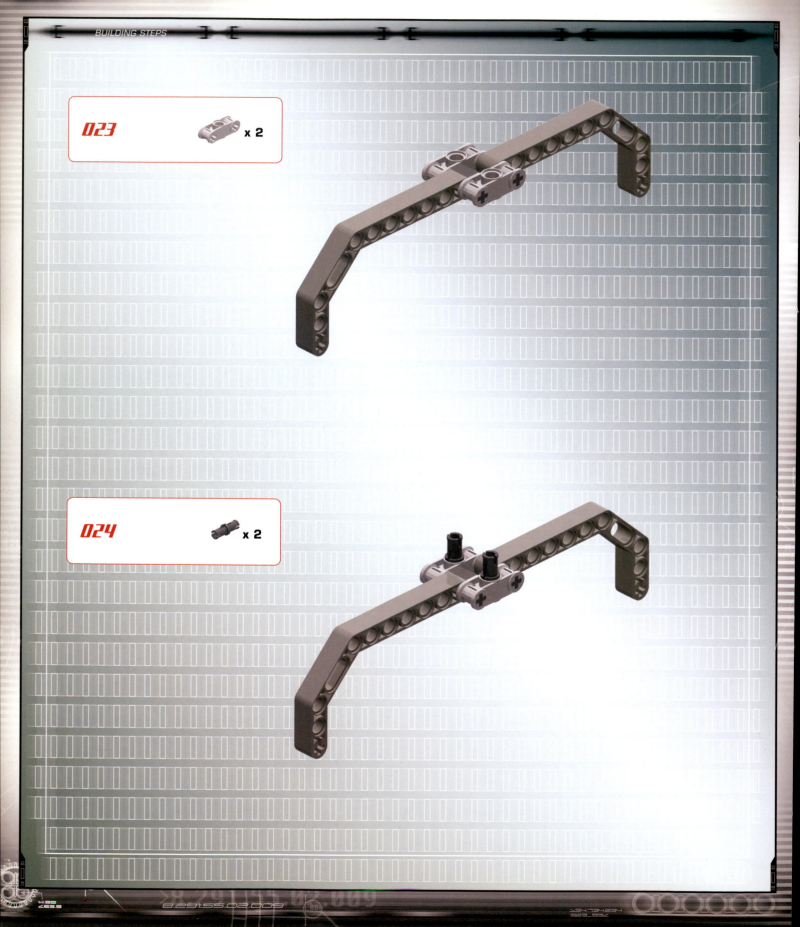

025 2M x 2

026 x 2

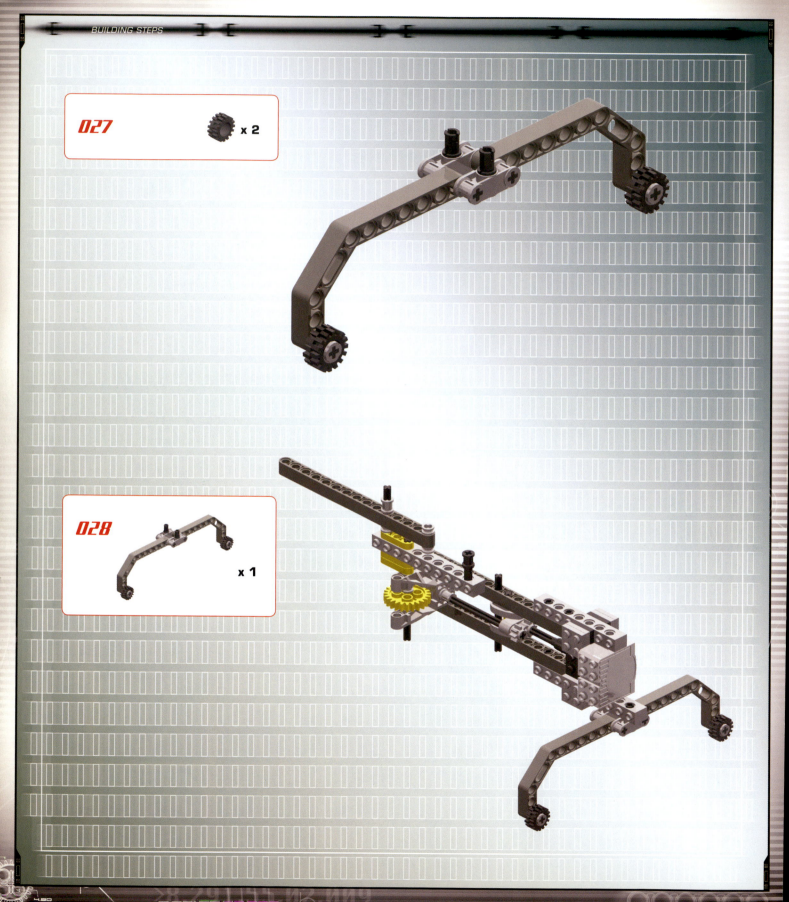

027   x 2

028   x 1

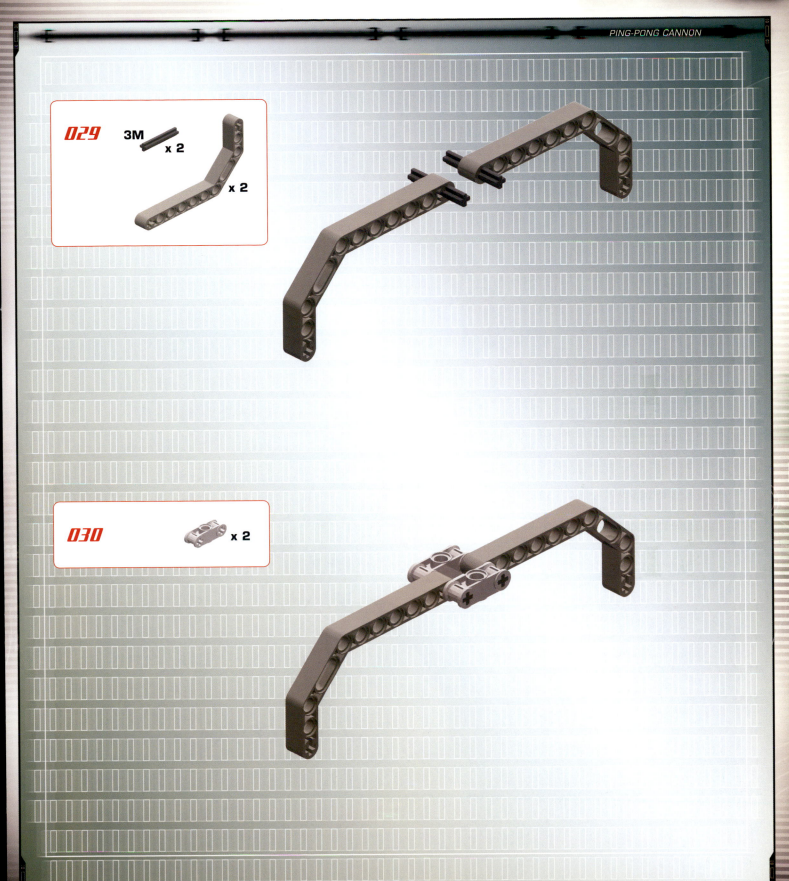

029
3M x 2
x 2

030
x 2

031 x 2

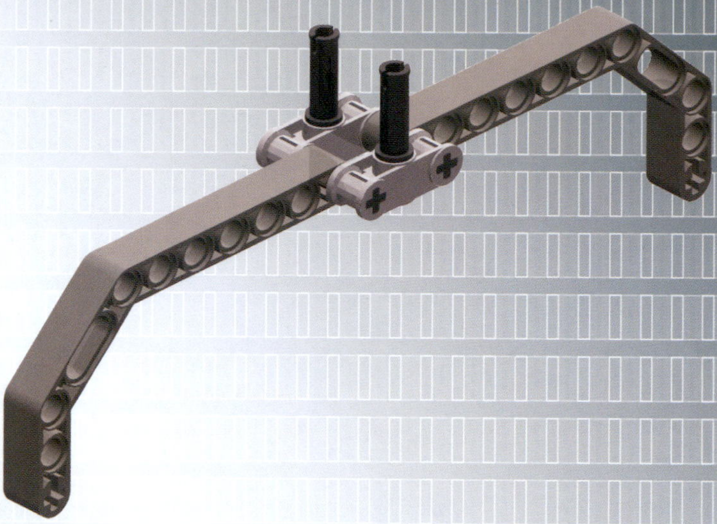

032 2M x 2

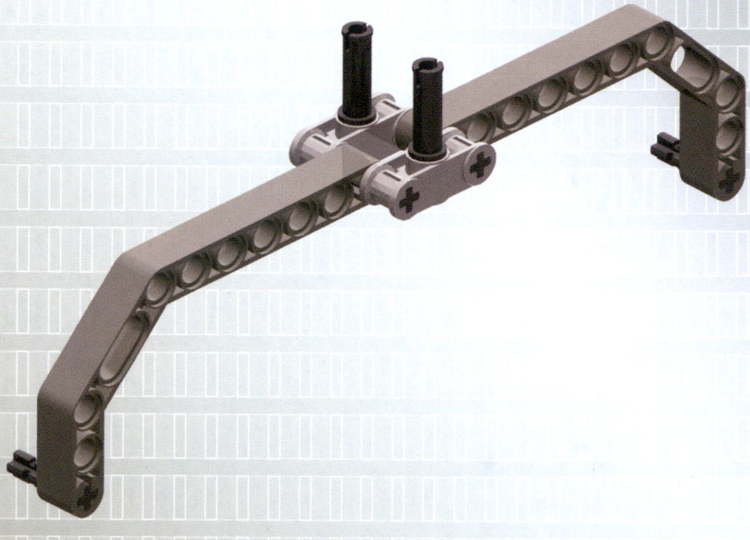

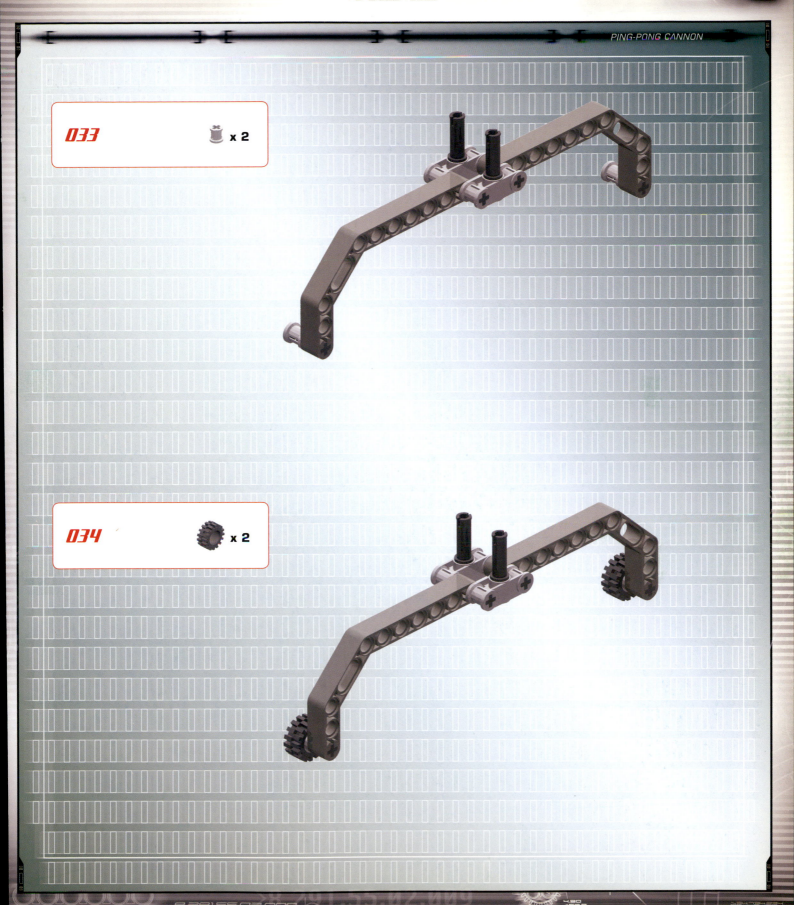

033 x 2

034 x 2

BUILDING STEPS

035 x 1

036 x 1

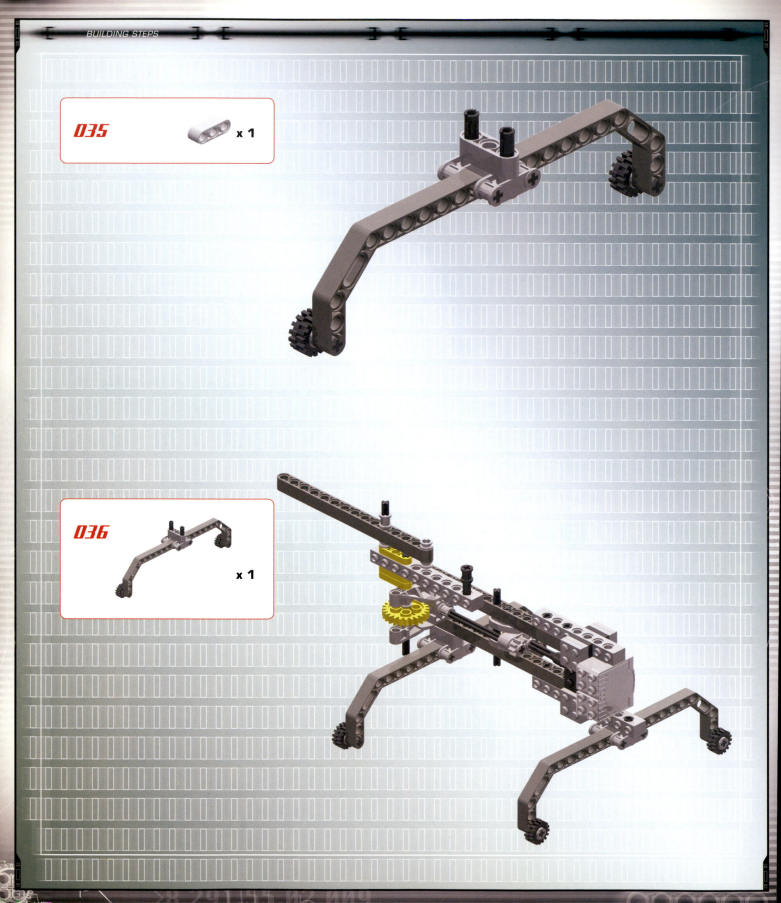

037 x 2

038 x 2

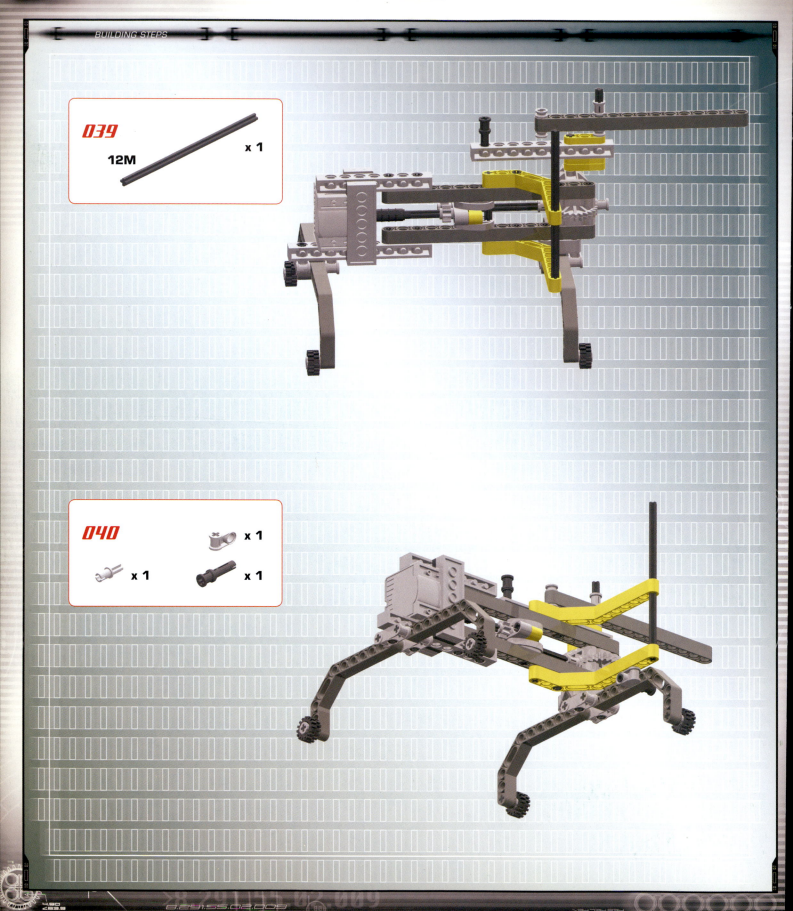

039

12M   x 1

040

x 1

x 1   x 1

041

x 1

x 3

042

x 1

x 1

043

x 1

x 1

044

x 1

x 2

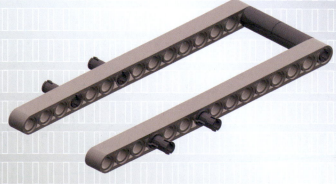

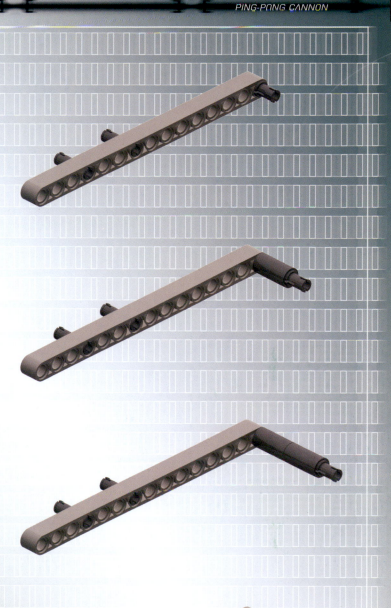

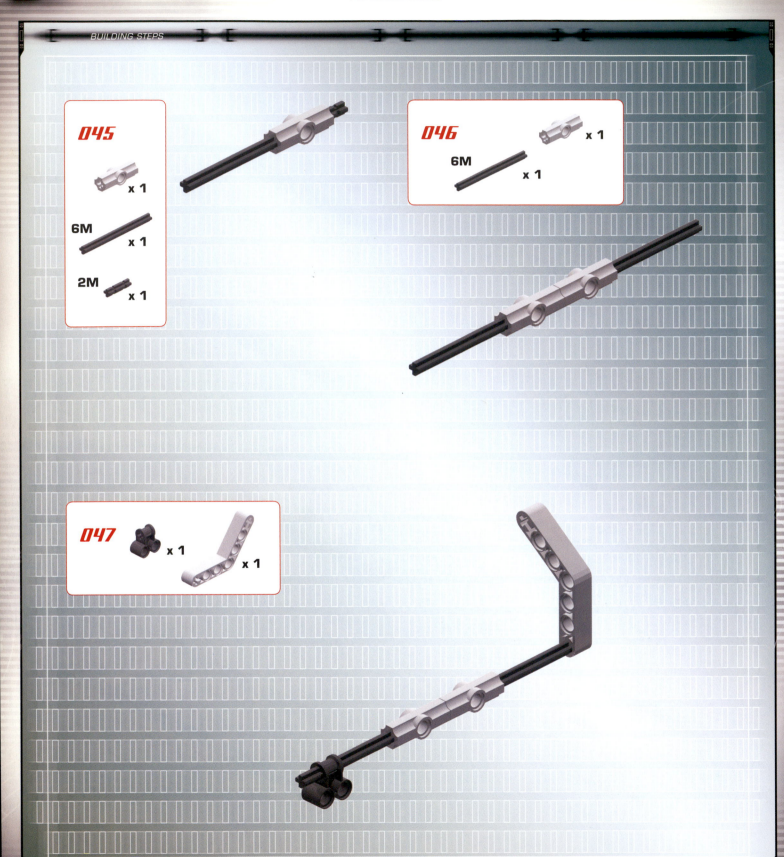

045

6M

2M

x 1

x 1

x 1

046

6M

x 1

x 1

047

x 1

x 1

048

x 1

x 1

049

x 2

050

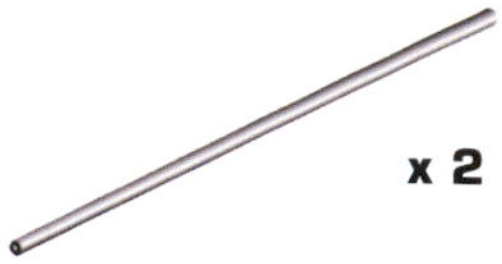

x 2

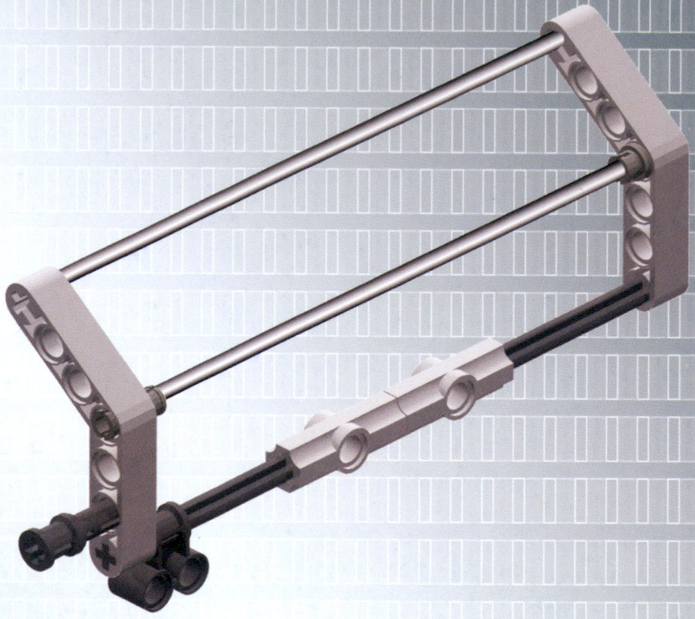

051

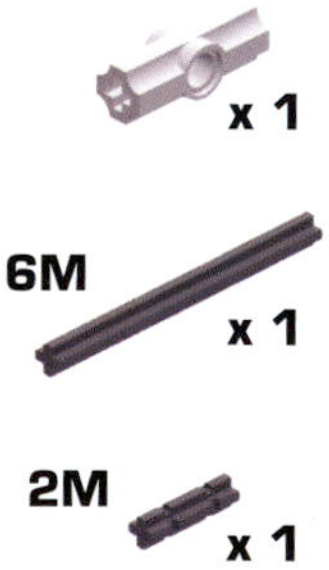

x 1

6M x 1

2M x 1

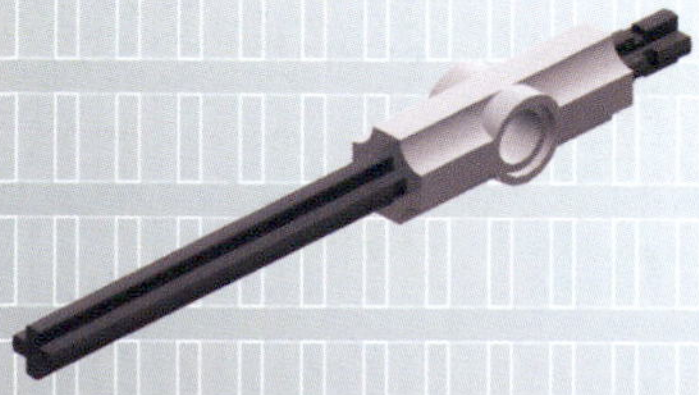

052

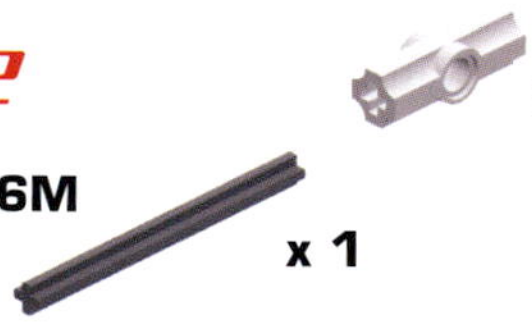

x 1

6M x 1

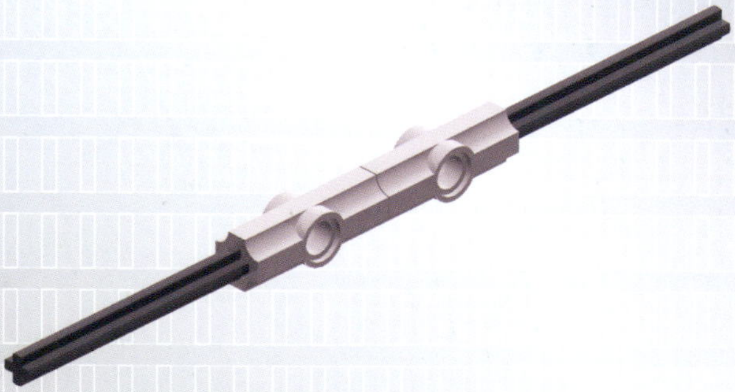

053 x 1 x 1

054 x 1 x 1

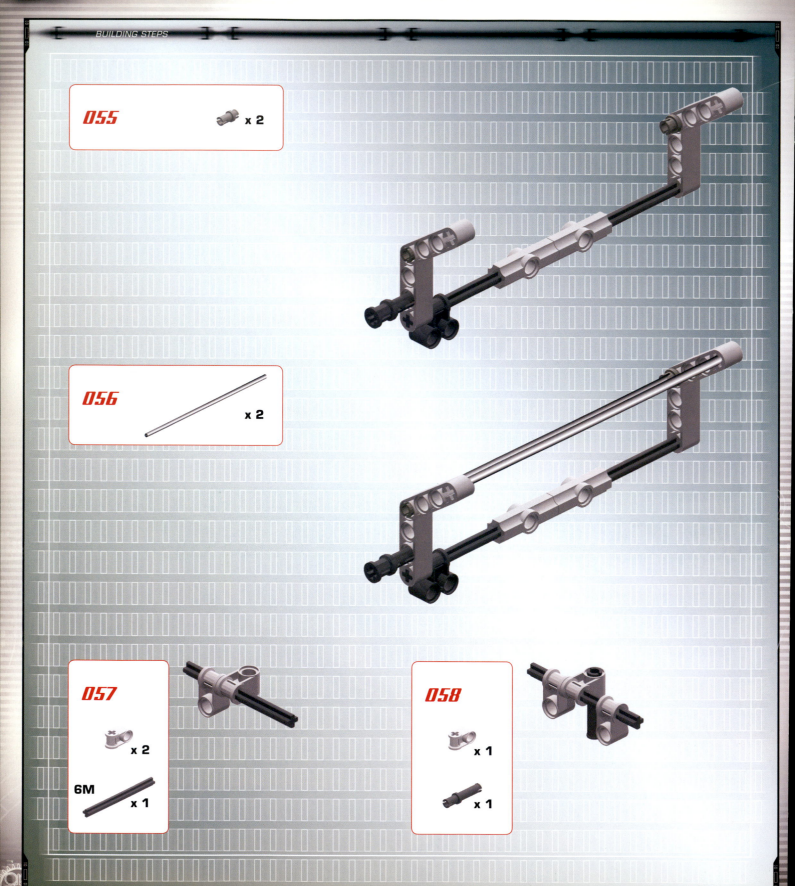

055 x 2

056 x 2

057 x 2
6M x 1

058 x 1
x 1

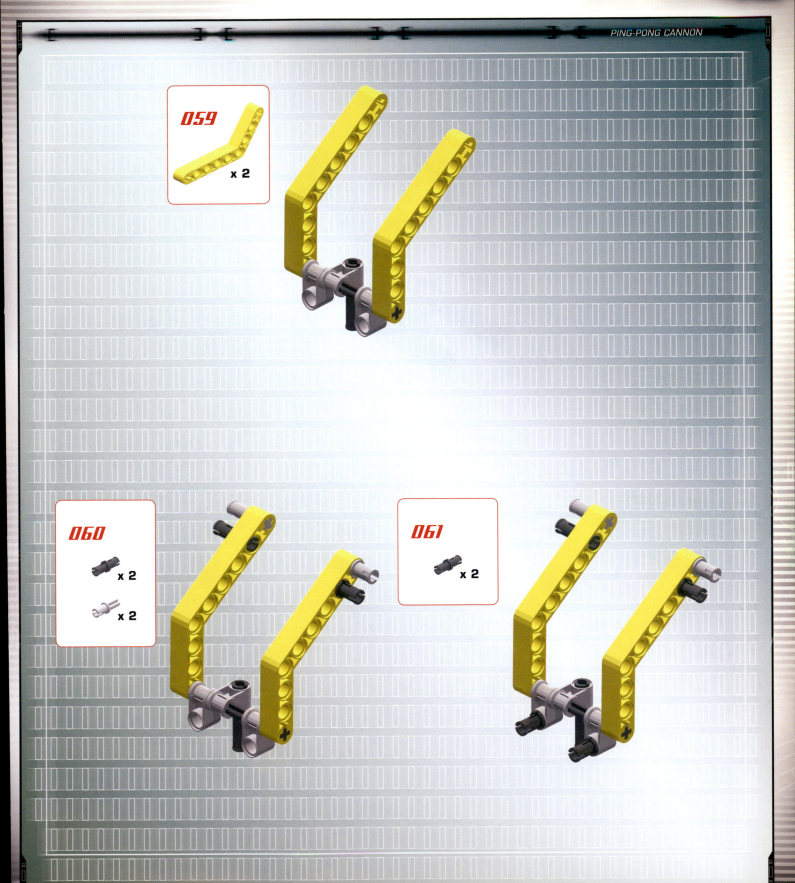

059 x 2

060 x 2 x 2

061 x 2

062

x 2

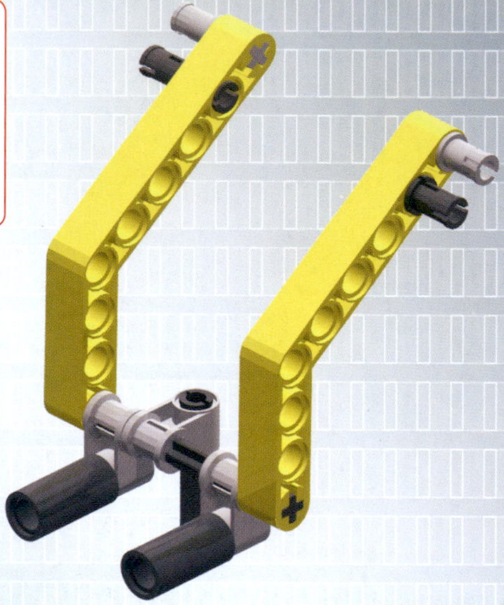

063

x 2

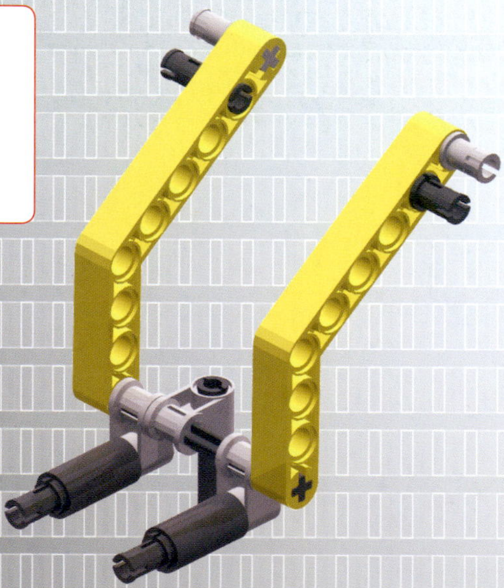

064

x 2

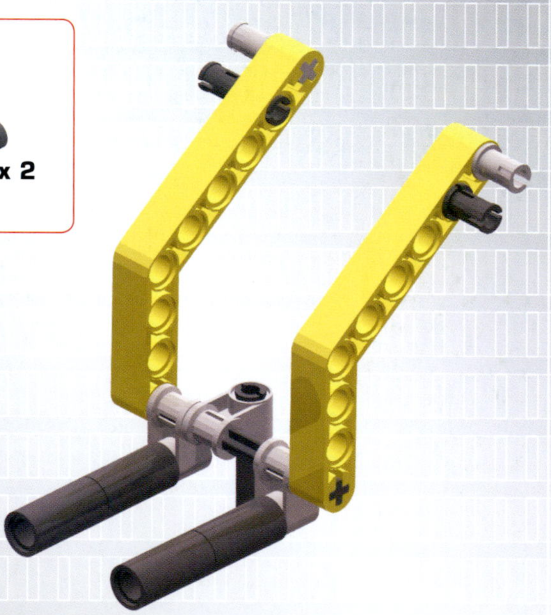

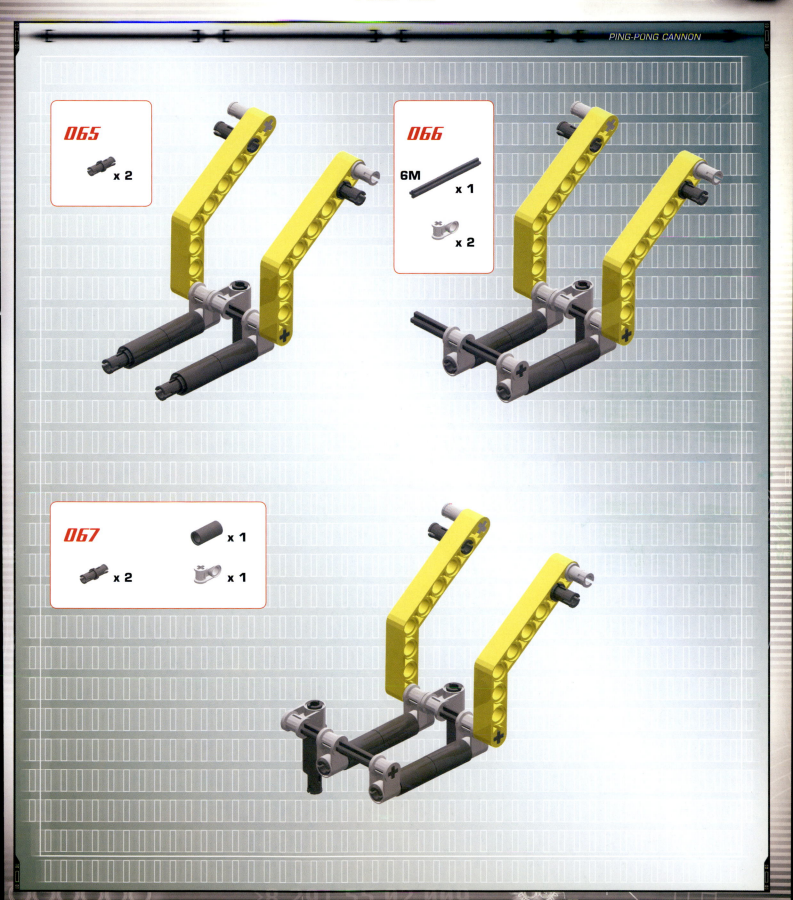

065
x 2

066
6M   x 1
x 2

067
x 1
x 2   x 1

068

x 1

x 1

x 1

069

x 1

070

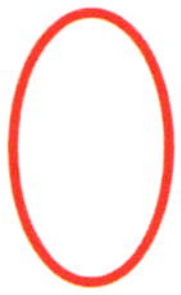

x 2

(rubber band)

PROJECT 4:
ALL-TERRAIN LEGO (ATL)

THE INSPIRATION

For a long time, Ulrik had to make do with only two springs in his LEGO collection—and they came from the Dune Buggy set (#8845) from 1981. He was always in need of more springs, especially when creating vehicles. As a result, he figured out how to use rubber bands instead of springs when developing vehicle suspensions. The rubber bands worked great, for a while. But over time they often weakened and snapped.

On the hunt for more springs, Ulrik took apart some pens and found that the springs inside them were nearly the same size as the ones needed for LEGO vehicles. With a little tweaking, a pen spring would fit right over a LEGO cross axle.

The ATL uses four springs, but if you don't have four LEGO springs, try disassembling some pens. You can almost always use items found around the house to create new stuff.

THE DESIGN

We used as many beams as possible to make the ATL incredibly durable, compact, and fast; it can serve as a driving platform for many different car models. The use of extra beams means you don't have to worry about the thing falling apart, even if you apply 18 volts to the motors—and you know you want to! (A 9V battery pack gives you a vehicle that performs decently, but double that to 18V, and this baby will fly.)

Since we wanted to design the model based on the 16 module TECHNIC beam, we had to modify axle lengths in order to keep the design compact. By using a 3 ½ module long axle, we were able to keep the vehicle as narrow as possible without having to remove its independent suspension.

Is it possible to destroy this model by driving it as hard as you can? Well, yes; it is only plastic, after all. But we have made it darn tough to destroy it! You will enjoy this durable model for a long time.

LEGO RULES BROKEN

To build the ATL, you will need to modify some of your LEGO pieces. Although LEGO designers alter pieces regularly in order to quickly visualize a concept, doing so is "officially" against LEGO rules. If the concept is subsequently chosen, the designers spend time altering the design slightly so that the model can be built using existing LEGO elements, or if that is impossible, they propose the creation of a new LEGO piece.

In order to maximize your ATL's power, see the Tips and Tricks chapter for the formula on how to get 18V out of two 9V LEGO battery packs. You really should do the 18 volt trick—an all-terrain LEGO vehicle with only 9 volts of power is sort of like a big SUV with a four-cylinder engine. And 18V makes driving through a wall of LEGO bricks even more fun! Of course, doubling the voltage applied to your vehicle breaks the official LEGO rules. But don't worry: Since the LEGO TECHNIC gear motor is so well constructed, it will handle the extra power without problems.

NON-LEGO PARTS USED

You do not need to add any non-LEGO parts to this model, but you'll get maximum clearance and traction if you use balloon or big tires, and by using two motors to steer (one for each wheel pair), you gain 100 percent control over your tank.

note: *Did you know that LEGO is actually the number one tire manufacturer in Europe? Granted, LEGO tires are a lot smaller than the tires most other companies produce, but LEGO still has them all beat on numbers. If you doubt us, check out your own LEGO collection and see how many tires you have between all of your sets.*

For easy turning on thick carpet, put plastic slicks on the front wheels. If you don't have any LEGO slicks or plastic wheels, wrap tape around the wheels to make them slip a bit so you can turn the vehicle more easily. Try it!

ALL-TERRAIN LEGO

If you're looking for a four-wheel drive vehicle that's capable of handling lots of power, this is the model for you! Using the cross locking strength of LEGO beams, the All Terrain LEGO (ATL) is a durable driving machine for all sorts of terrain, and independent suspension on each wheel ensures that you have maximum traction. Not only is this chassis lightweight, good looking, and darn cool, it will take all the power you can provide and convert it into pure brute driving force. If LEGO made life-size bricks and parts, you could build this puppy large enough to get in and take it for a spin in the country—watch out, Range Rover!

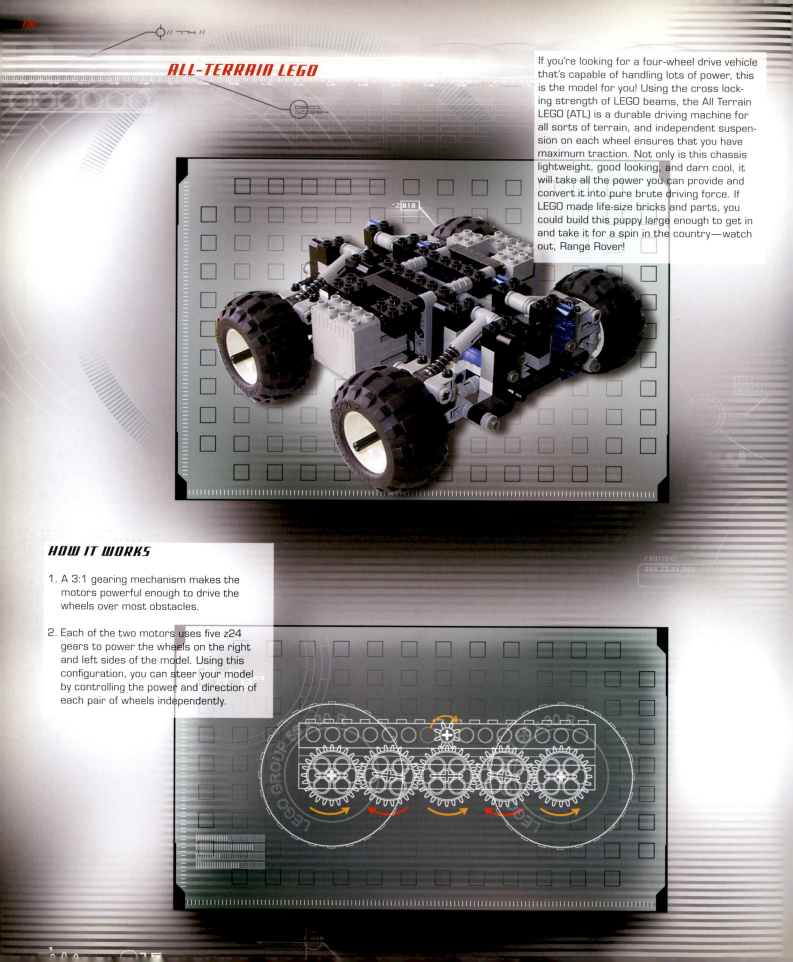

HOW IT WORKS

1. A 3:1 gearing mechanism makes the motors powerful enough to drive the wheels over most obstacles.

2. Each of the two motors uses five z24 gears to power the wheels on the right and left sides of the model. Using this configuration, you can steer your model by controlling the power and direction of each pair of wheels independently.

2M x 8

3M x 2

4M x 22

5M x 4

6M x 4

x 24

x 4

x 24

x 16

x 2

x 2

x 40

x 4

x 8

x 16

x 4

x 2

x 16

x 8

x 8

x 8

x 2

x 4

x 4

x 4

x 10

x 24

x 8

x 2

x 8

x 4

x 6

x 20

x 8

x 4

x 4

x 4

x 4

ALL-TERRAIN LEGO TIP

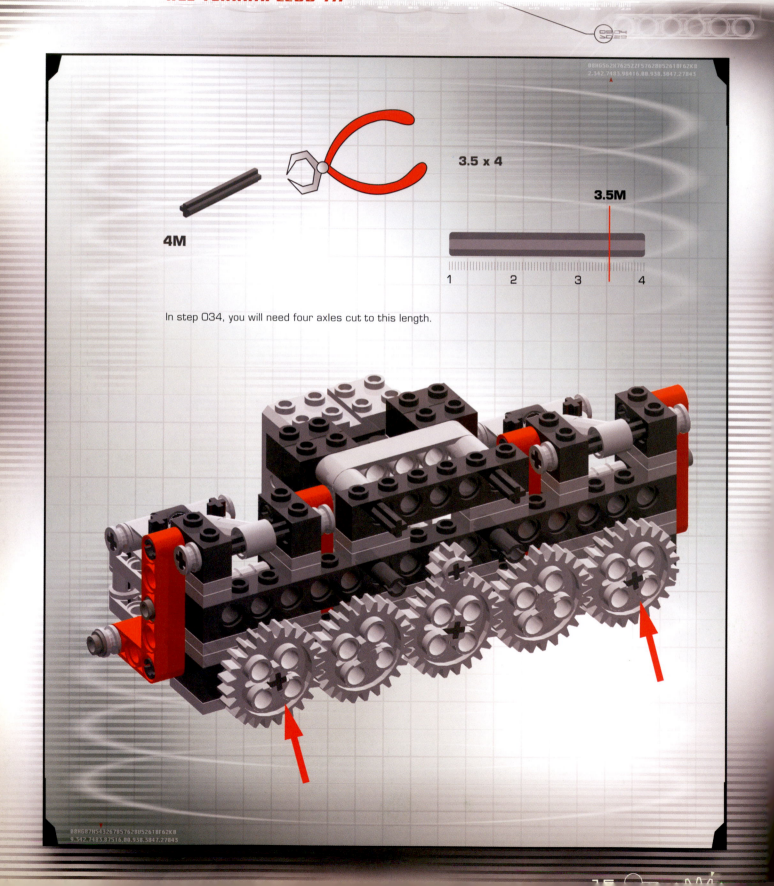

4M

3.5 x 4

3.5M

1   2   3   4

In step 034, you will need four axles cut to this length.

BBHG562H7625ZZF57628U52618F62K8
2.342.7483.98416.88.938.5847.27843

ALL TERRAIN LEGO

001

x 1

x 4

NOTE: To make both sides of the vehicle, you will ultimately need two copies of the assembly you're about to build in steps 001 through 051. Whether you build them both concurrently or one at a time is up to you.

002

 x 4

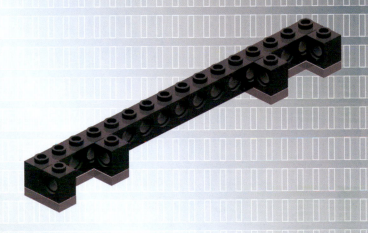

003

 x 4

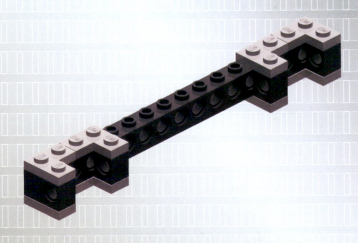

004 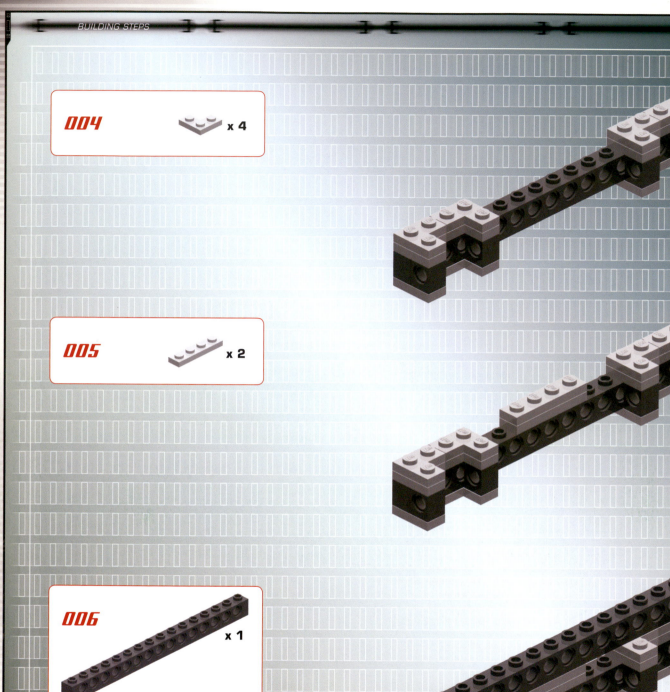 x 4

005 x 2

006 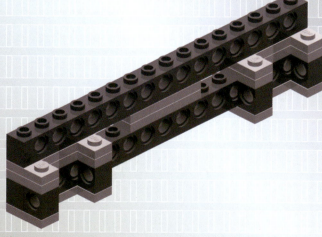 x 1

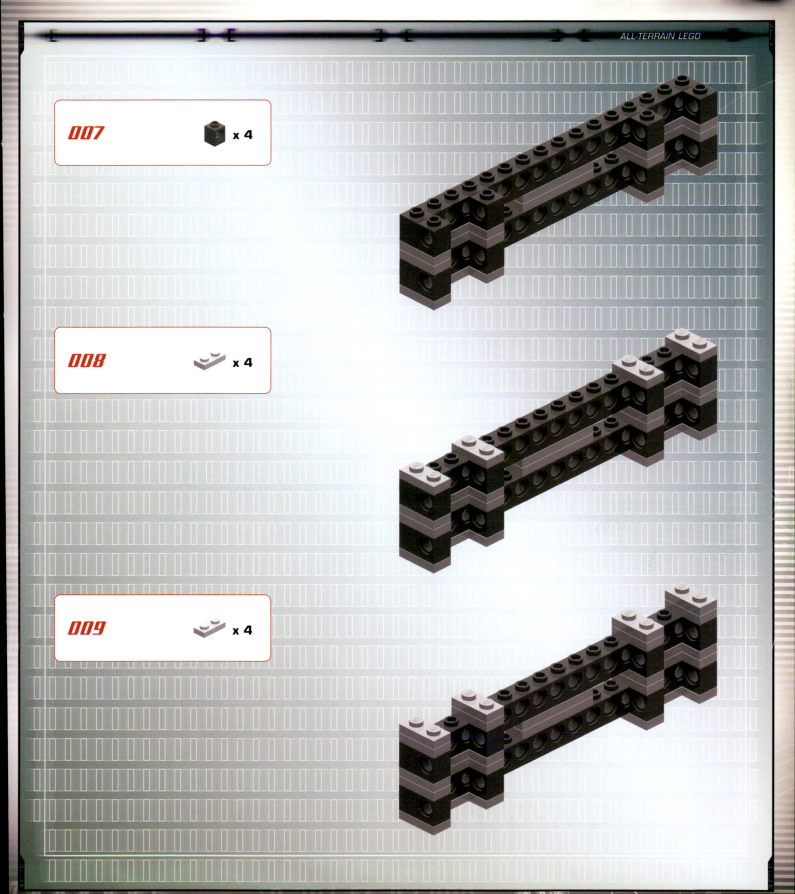

007 x 4

008 x 4

009 x 4

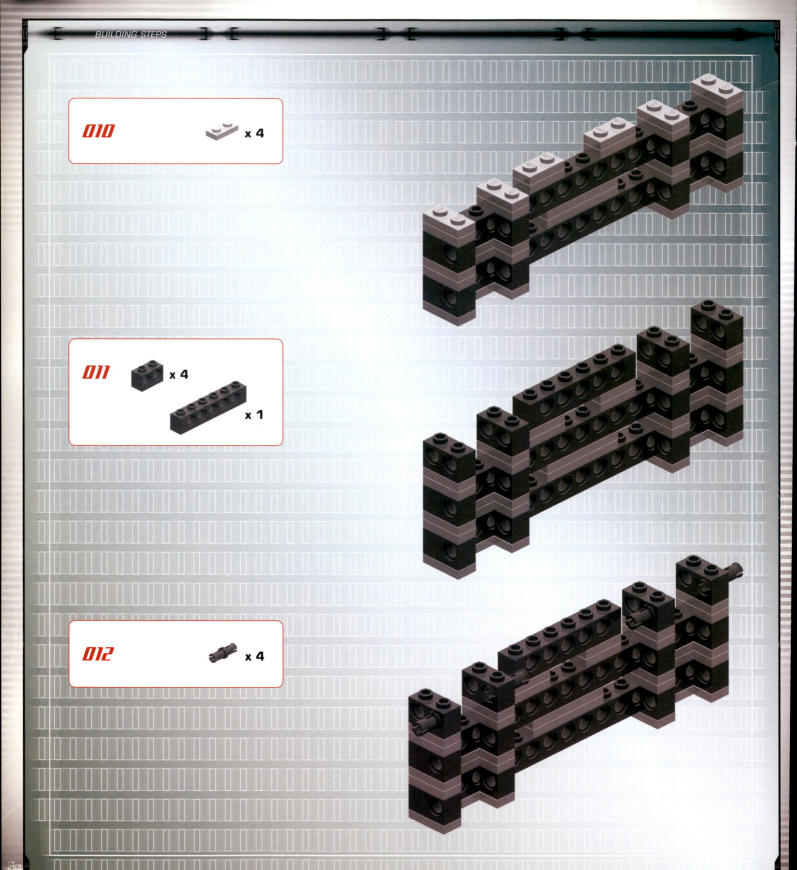

010 x 4

011 x 4
x 1

012 x 4

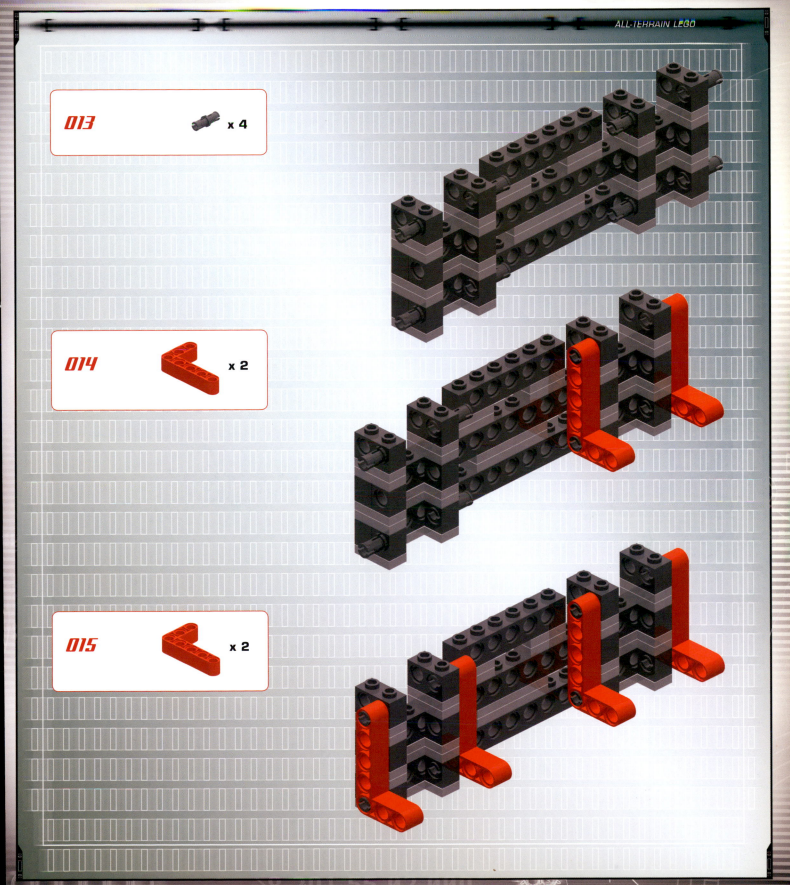

013 x 4

014 x 2

015 x 2

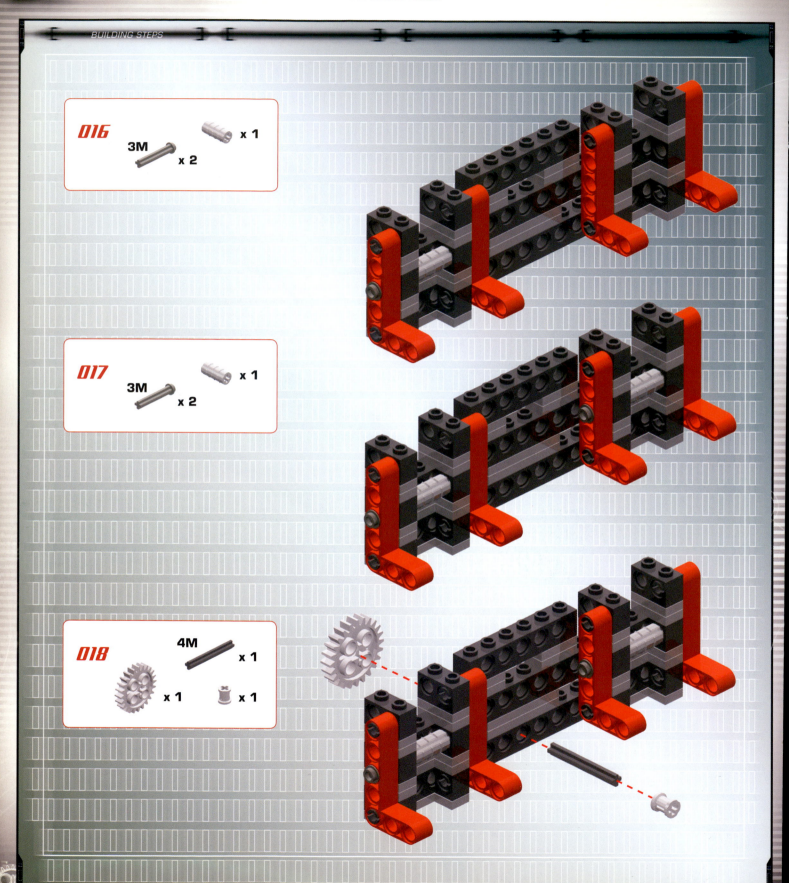

016

3M x 2

x 1

017

3M x 2

x 1

018

4M x 1

x 1

x 1

019

020 x 2

021 x 2

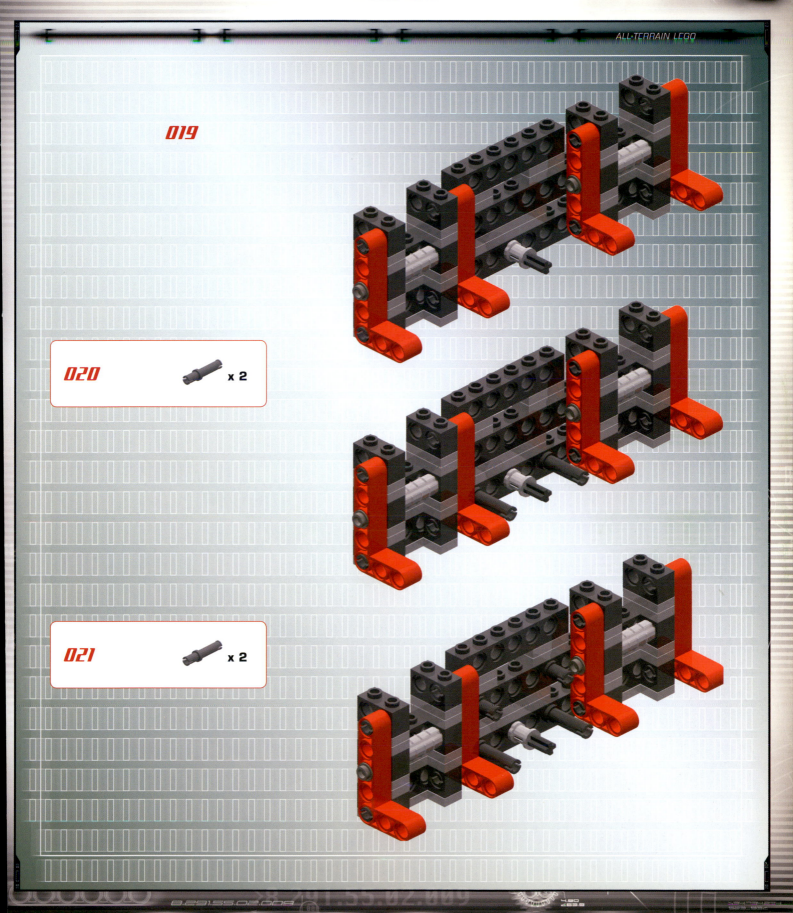

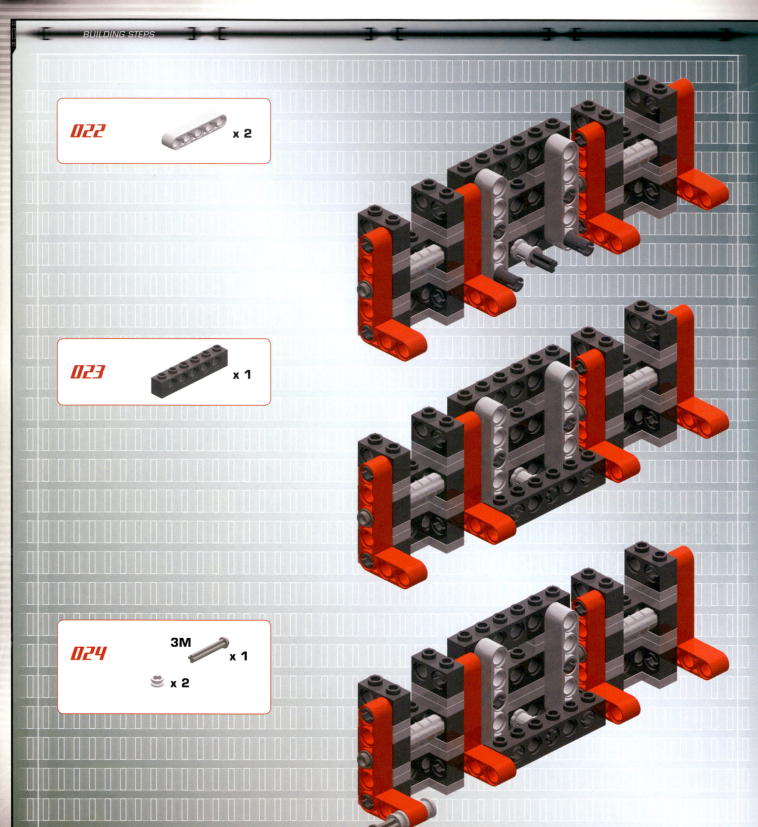

022 x 2

023 x 1

024 3M x 1 x 2

025

3M x 1

x 2

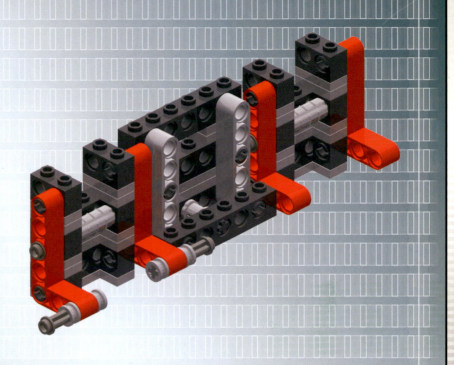

026

3M x 2

x 4

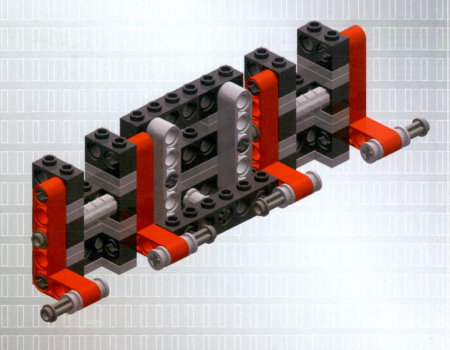

027

x 1

2M
x 2

note: For each side of the vehicle, you will need two copies of the assembly you're about to build in steps 027 through 035. (That means you'll ultimately need to build four copies of this assembly.)

028

x 2

029

4M
x 2

030

x 2

031

x 2

032

x 1

033

 x 2

034

 x 1

3.5M* x 1

 x 2

4M x 1

* Use the cut axles you created from the Tip instructions at the beginning of this project.

035

 x 1

036

 x 1

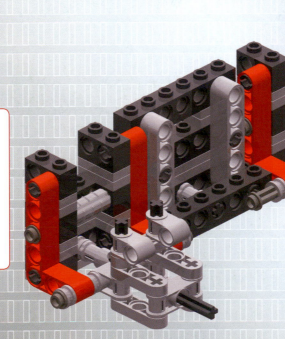

037 x 1

If you haven't done so already, go back to step 027 and repeat the steps up to step 035 to build another copy of this assembly. Attach it as shown in this step, then proceed to step 038.

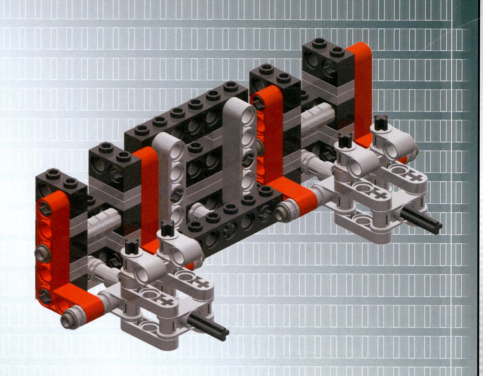

038

4M x 1

5M x 1

x 1

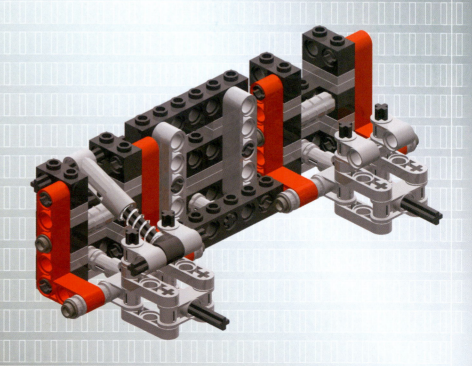

039

 x 4

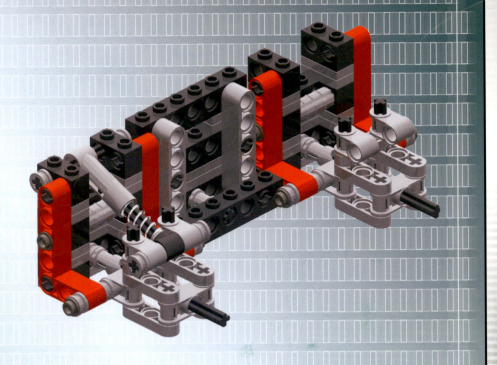

040

4M x 1

5M x 1

x 1

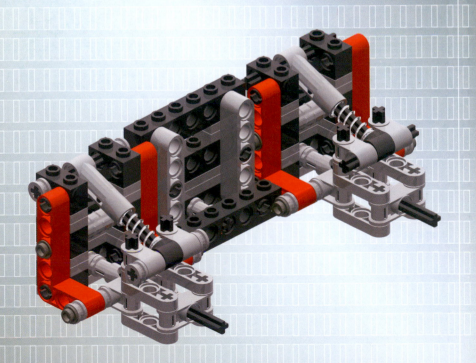

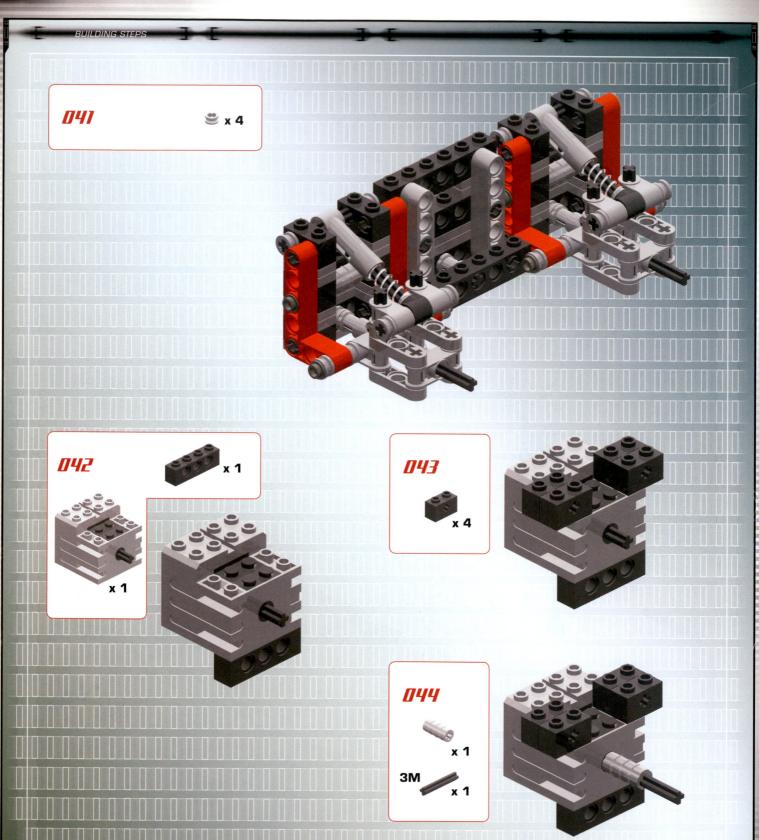

041 x 4

042 x 1 / x 1

043 x 4

044 x 1 / 3M x 1

045

6M x 2

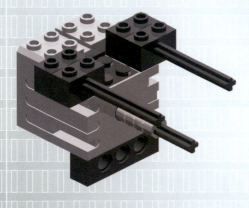

046

x 2

x 1

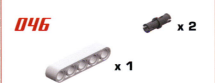

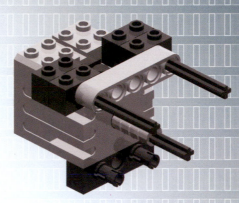

047

x 1

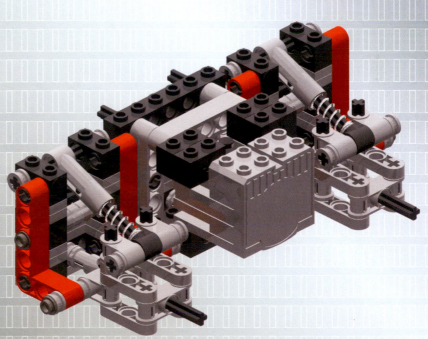

048 x 1

049 x 2

050 x 2

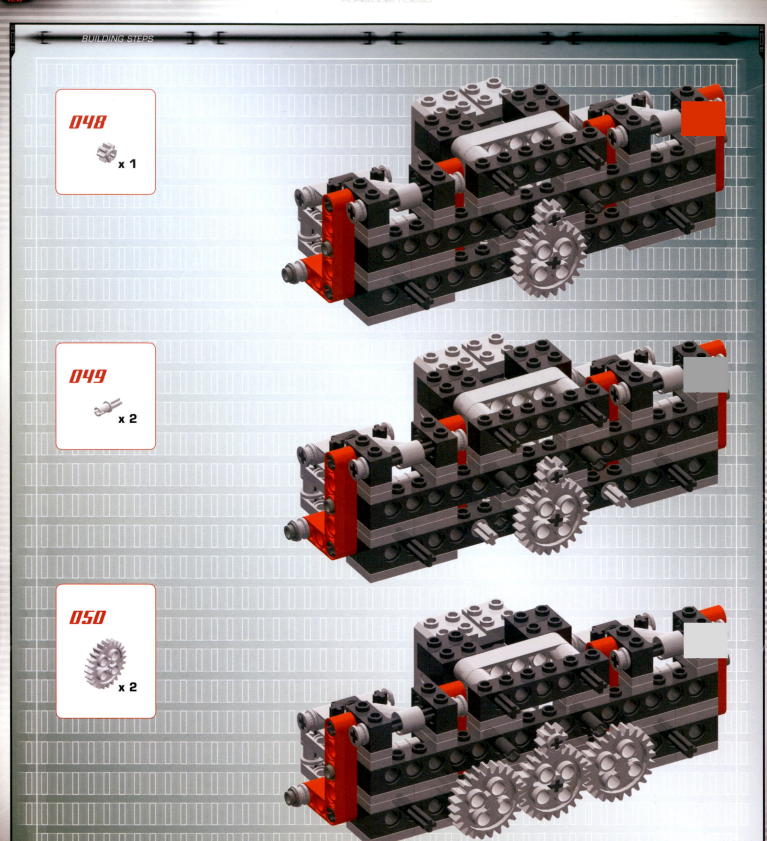

051

x 2

If you haven't been building two copies of this assembly concurrently, you now need to go back to step 001 and build another copy. Then proceed to step 052.

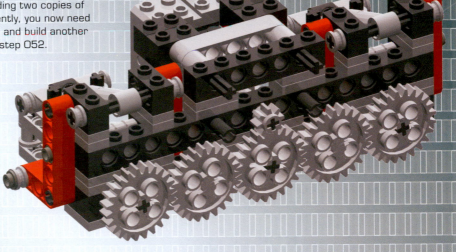

052

x 2

x 2

x 2

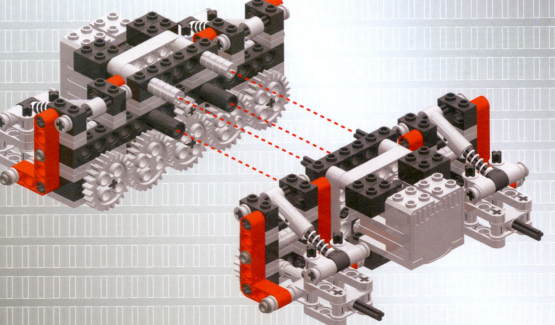

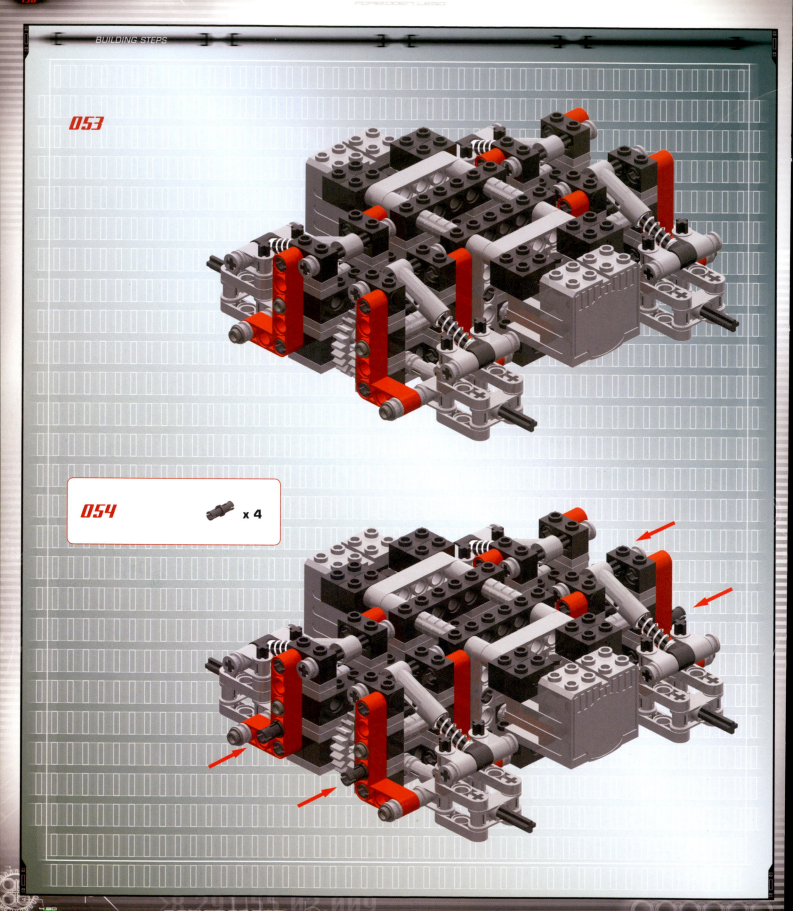

053

054 x 4

055

x 4

056 x 4

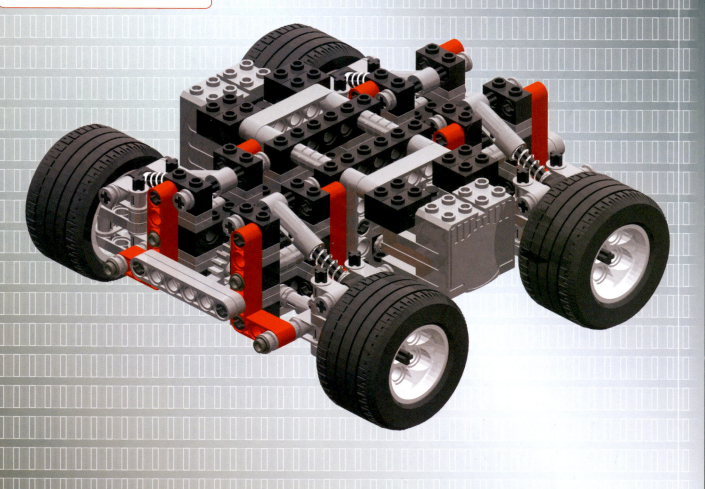

PROJECT 5:
HIGH VELOCITY AUTOMATIC LEGO PLATE DISPENSER (HVALPD)

OVERVIEW

Yes, this sweet machine will fire off a round of 14 LEGO roof plates in less than eight seconds! Just squeeze the trigger and the force of the dual in-line LEGO motor power plant and rubber-band-driven ramming beam will automatically empty the magazine with amazing speed and precision—and generate some great sound effects too!

But beware: The High Velocity Automatic LEGO Plate Dispenser (HVALPD) breaks so many LEGO rules that you should proceed with great caution. Please use this model only for the peaceful and constructive dispensing of plates—like when you're laying out a patio for the back of your Belleville model playhouse and you just need to get those pink 1 x 8 plates out as fast possible.

THE INSPIRATION

This model shows how versatile and great the LEGO TECHNIC line is, proving that you can build whatever you want and get the contraption to look really cool, too. This model is also the one that is most true to the title of this book—it violates lots of LEGO rules, including the granddaddy of them all: modifying bricks by cutting and gluing them. You'll have to do a bit of brick adjusting before you can fully enjoy the mechanics of the HVALPD. But don't worry—it will all be explained in the building instructions section. And if you're worried about modifying your LEGO bricks, remember that you can always buy more in accessory packs from LEGO.com or in LEGO stores.

THE DESIGN

The key design issue here is striking the right balance between the force of the motors and the force of the rubber bands. The force of the motors must be stronger than that of the rubber bands in order to pull the beam back to the launching position. At the same time, the rubber bands must have enough strength to pull the beam forward with as much force as possible when released. This is why adding two motors and even doubling the voltage improves the performance. Stronger motors + stronger rubber bands = more launching force.

The HVALPD is the ultimate in extreme LEGO building. It not only pushes well beyond the limits of the official LEGO rules, but it does so elegantly. When you build this model you will find that everything fits together so perfectly and works so effectively that it's hard not to imagine that LEGO engineers originally designed the parts to be used this way. If you don't believe us, try building a model like this with K'NEX. You should quickly grasp the difference between a set of plastic toy pieces that stick together and a full building system that lets you design and construct real, working inventions.

You can stack up to 14 1 x 8 roof plates into this model's magazine. The cross axle on top is there to make sure that the plates don't fall out while you run around trying to aim at your next non-human, non-animal target.

note: *Be careful when you test this model because parts may fly in different directions. We strongly recommend that you wear goggles or some other protective eyewear for safety.*

One motor alone couldn't do the job, so we put in two! Now, while this model will work with a 9V battery box, the real fun starts when you apply 18V to the system and add more rubber bands to add more power. (Don't worry; your LEGO pieces can take the stress.)

note: *See the Tips and Tricks chapter for more information on getting 18 volts out of two 9V LEGO battery packs.*

LEGO RULES BROKEN

Rules broken…what can we say? This design breaks so many LEGO rules that a list is more appropriate than a long boring paragraph that you wouldn't read anyway. So, here we go:

- Never launch a non-approved object into the air.

- Never launch a non-approved object into the air with great force.

- Never alter any LEGO part. (And definitely don't cut the teeth off of gears in a non-symmetrical pattern!)

- Never connect two motors to run together.

- Never double the approved voltage.

- Never use glue while building.

- Never follow the directions in this book again!

HIGH VELOCITY AUTOMATIC LEGO PLATE DISPENSER

HOW IT WORKS

1. The two motors use a 3:1 gearing ratio to turn the modified z24 gear wheel with a great deal of speed and force.

2. As the gear wheel turns, it pulls the ramming beam backward, and the rubber bands stretch and tug at the beam in the opposite direction.

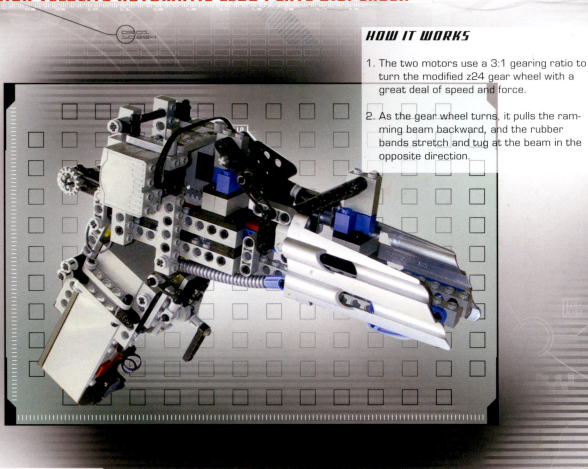

3. The launching position is reached when the z24 gear wheel rotates to the point where the teeth are missing, allowing the ramming beam to slip free.

4. The rubber bands snap back and pull the ramming beam forward to make it shoot out a plate.

5. The gear wheel turns a bit further until the teeth re-engage and pull the ramming beam back again, allowing another plate to fall into the launching chamber.

6. The process repeats, shooting one plate out with each full turn of the gear.

x 1

x 2

x 3

x 1

x 5

x 16

x 14

x 6

x 1

x 8

x 14

2M x 6

3M x 8

3M x 1

4M x 4

5M x 3

6M x 3

8M x 3

x 2

x 2

x 2

x 4

x 2

x 2

x 9

(rubber band)

x 2

x 2

x 2

x 1

x 1

x 2

x 2

x 2

x 2

x 2

x 2

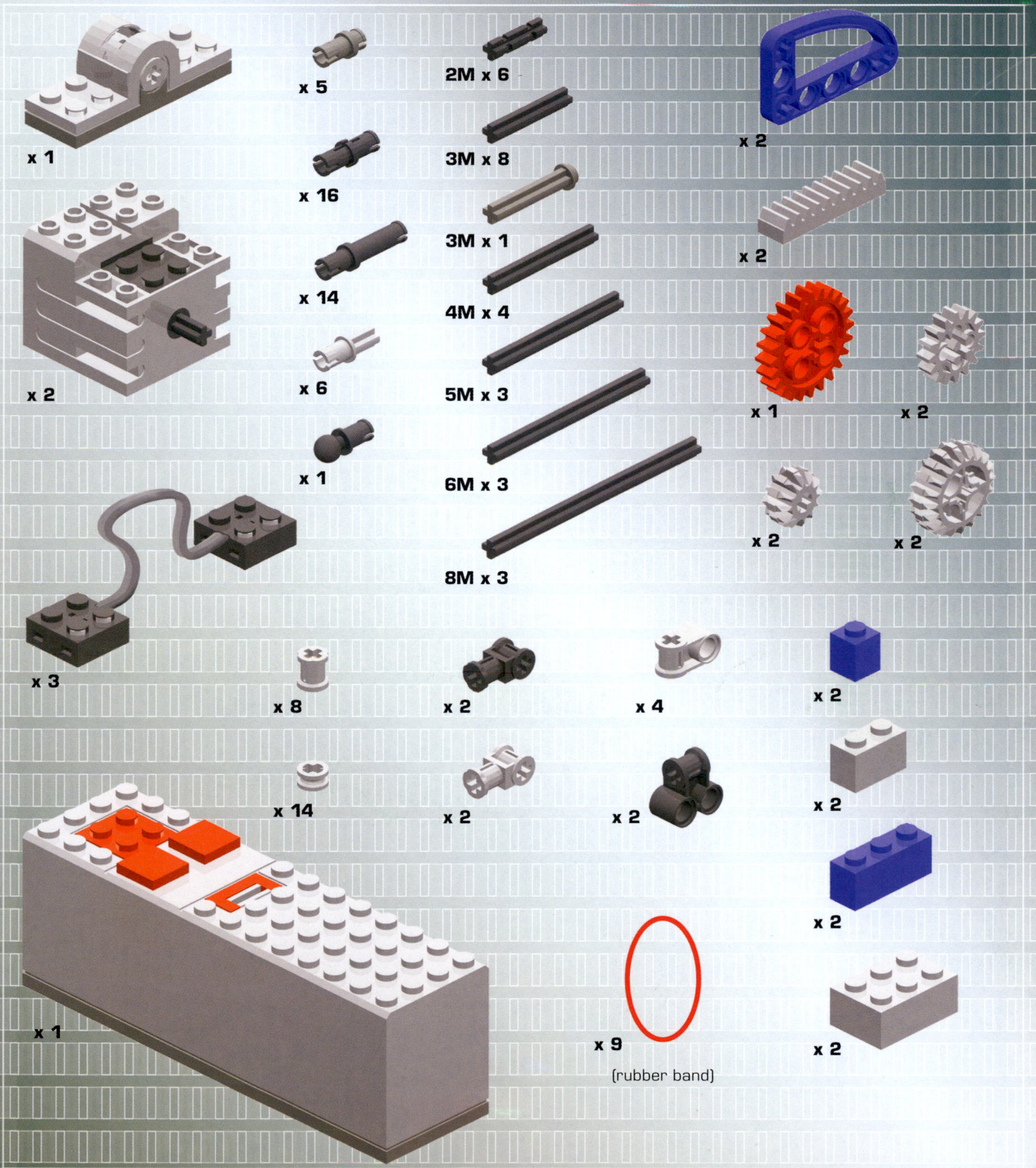

PARTS LIST

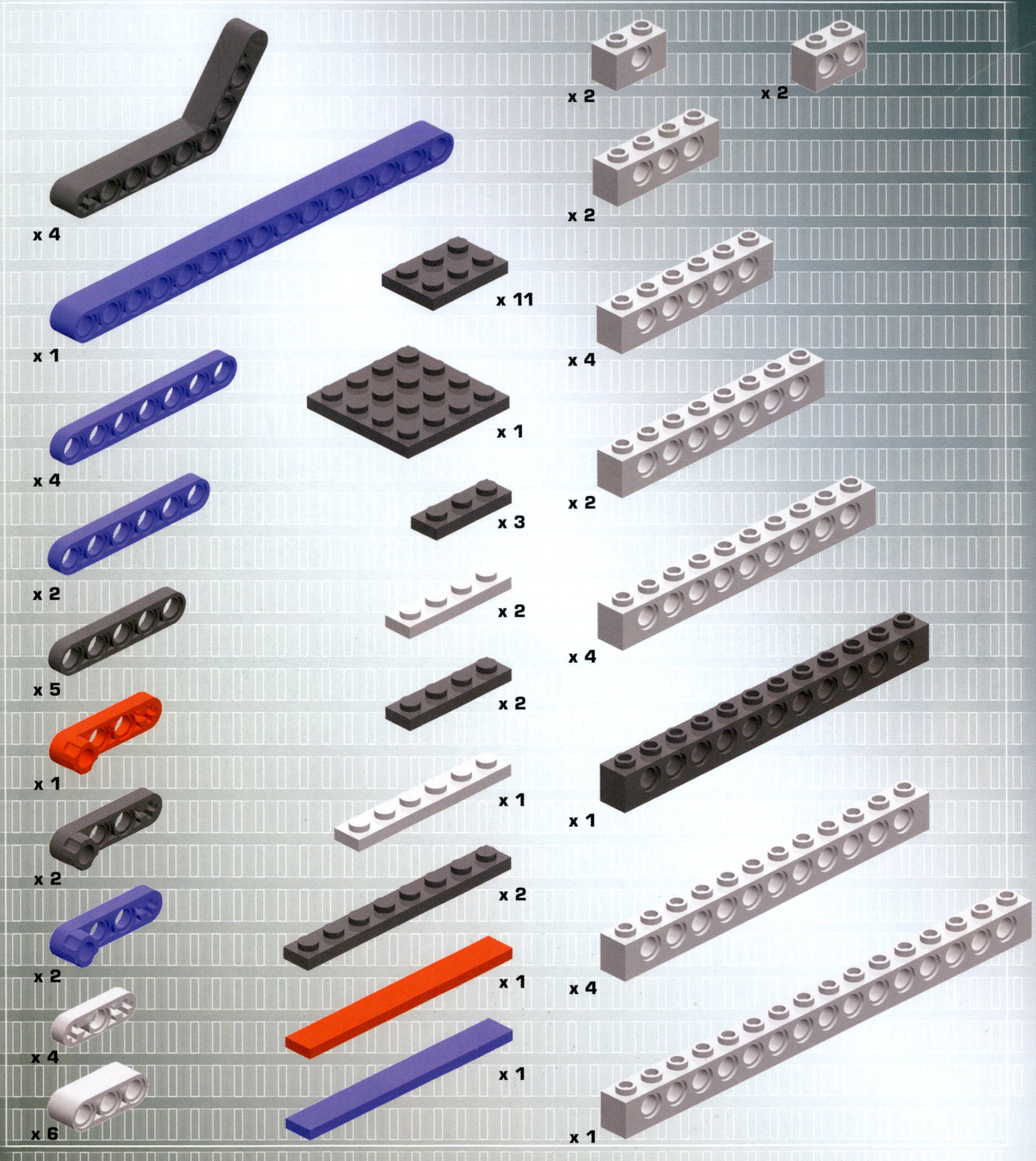
x 4
x 1
x 4
x 2
x 5
x 1
x 2
x 2
x 4
x 6
x 11
x 1
x 3
x 2
x 2
x 1
x 2
x 1
x 1
x 2
x 2
x 2
x 4
x 2
x 4
x 1
x 4
x 1

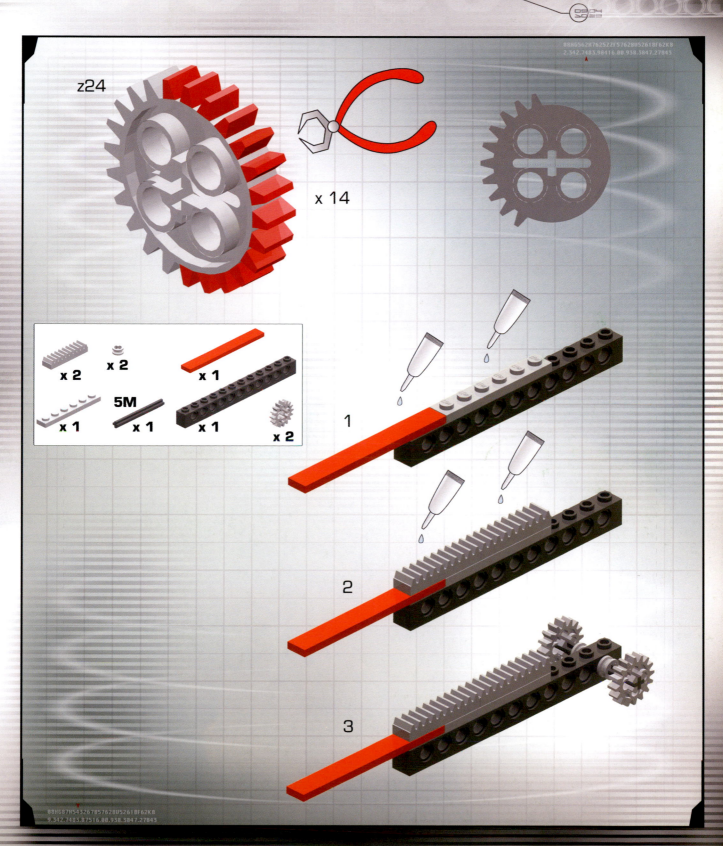

z24

x 14

x 2   x 2   x 1

5M

x 1   x 1   x 1   x 2

1

2

3

001

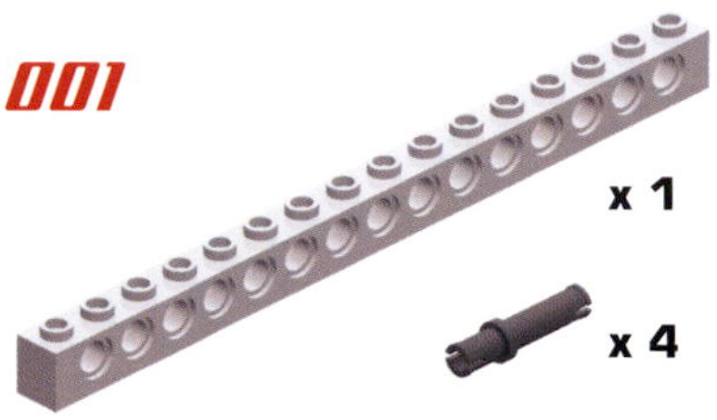

x 1

x 4

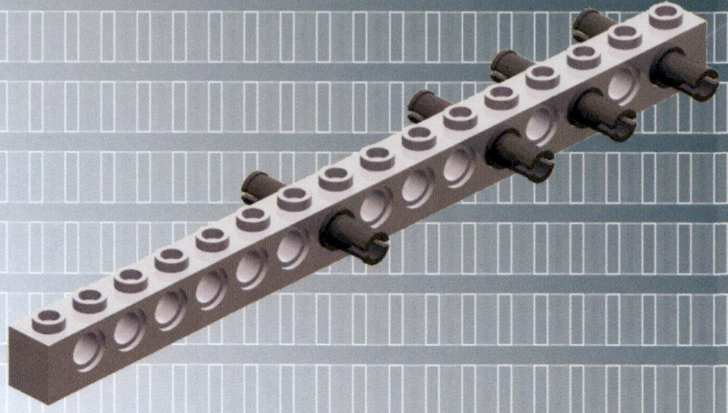

002

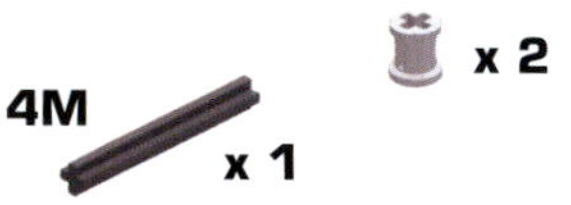

4M

x 1

x 2

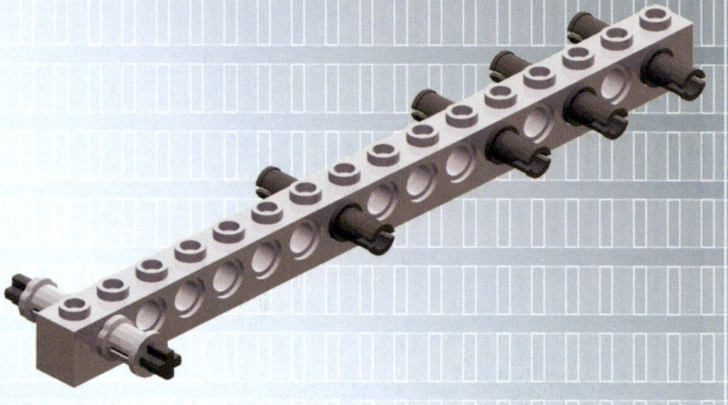

003

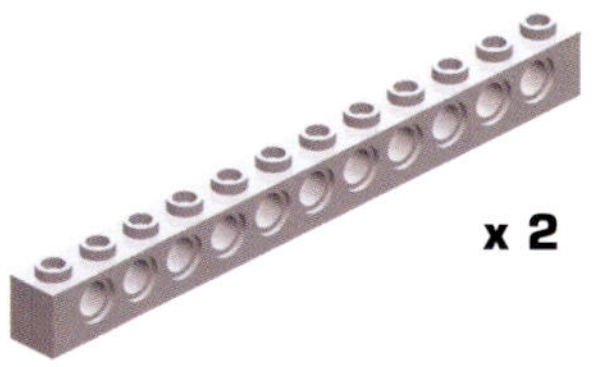

x 2

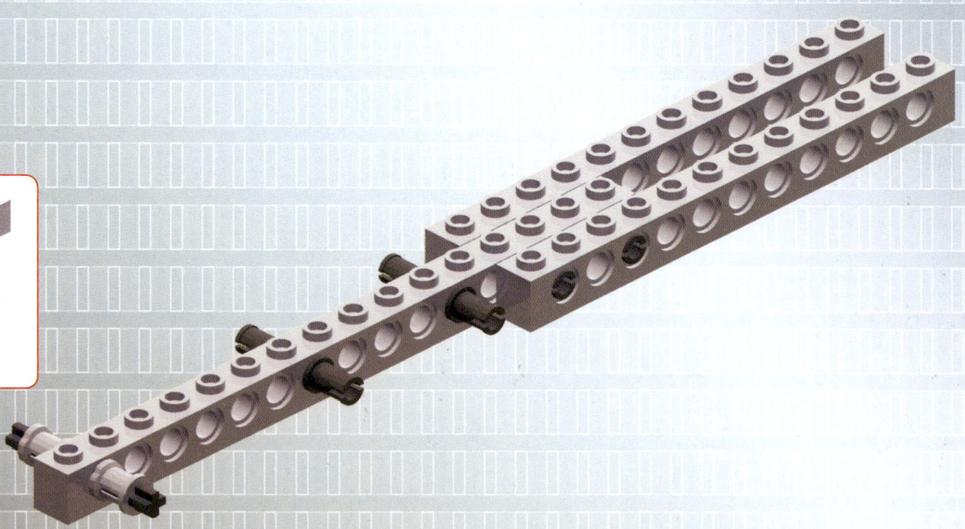

004 x 4

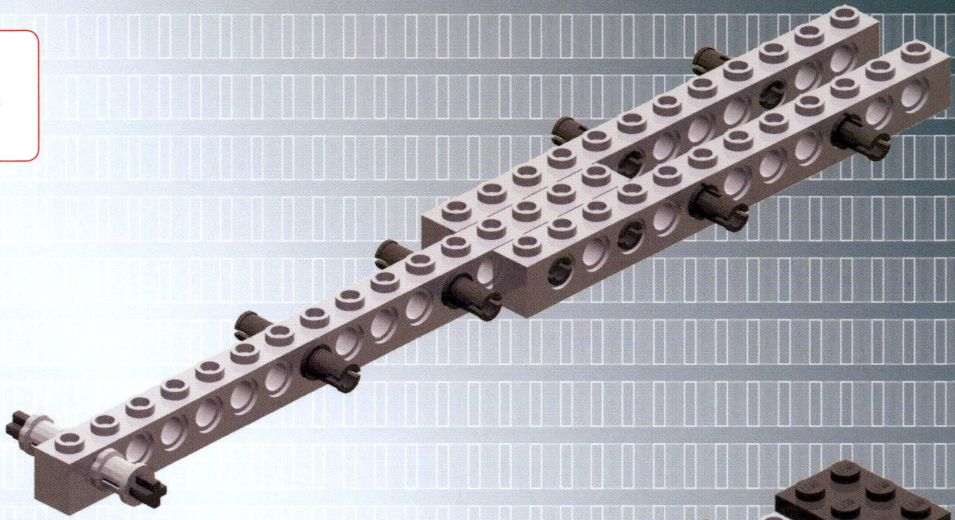

005 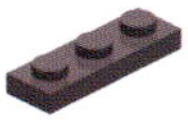 x 1
x 4 

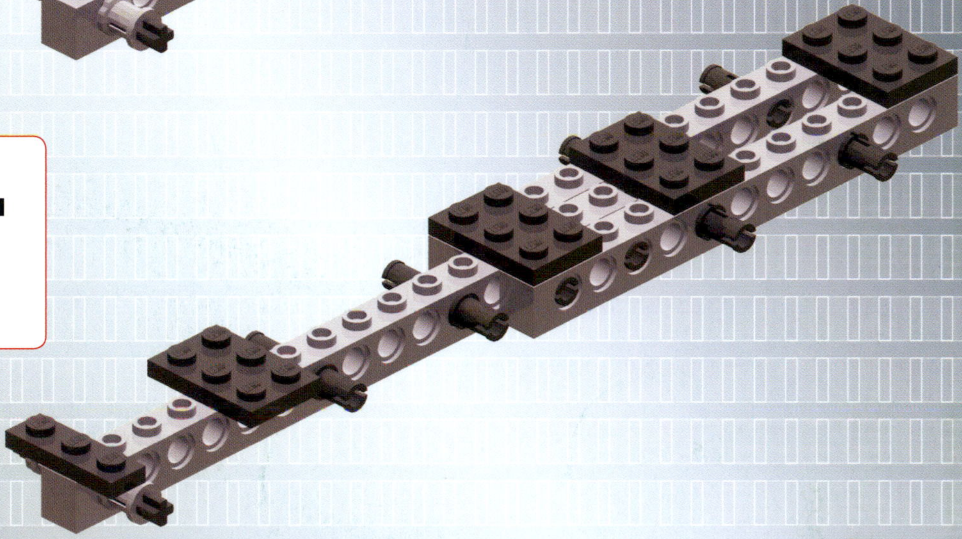

006  x 3

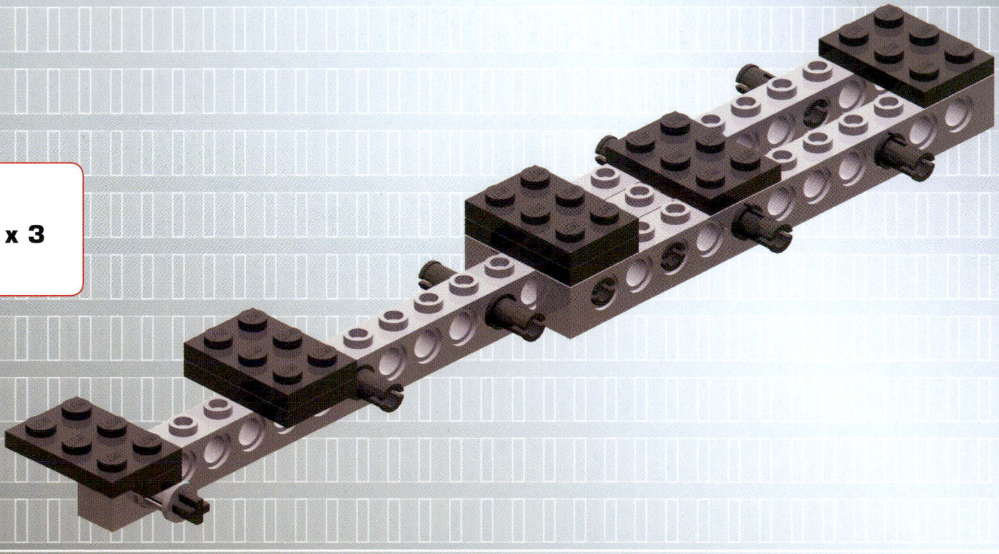

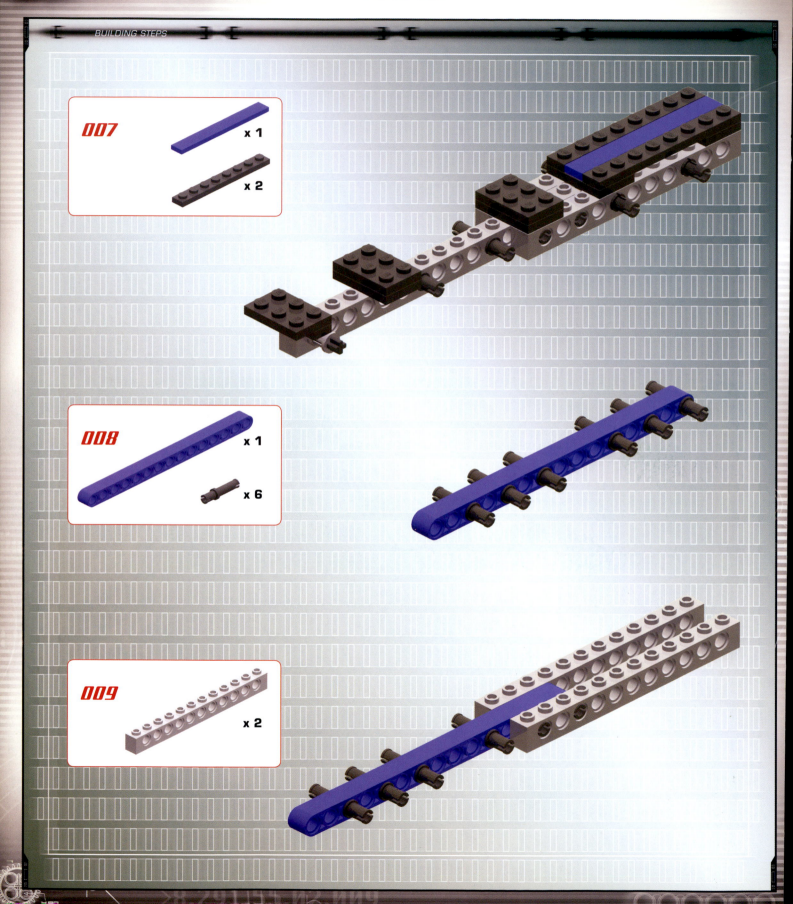

007

x 1

x 2

008

x 1

x 6

009

x 2

010

x 2

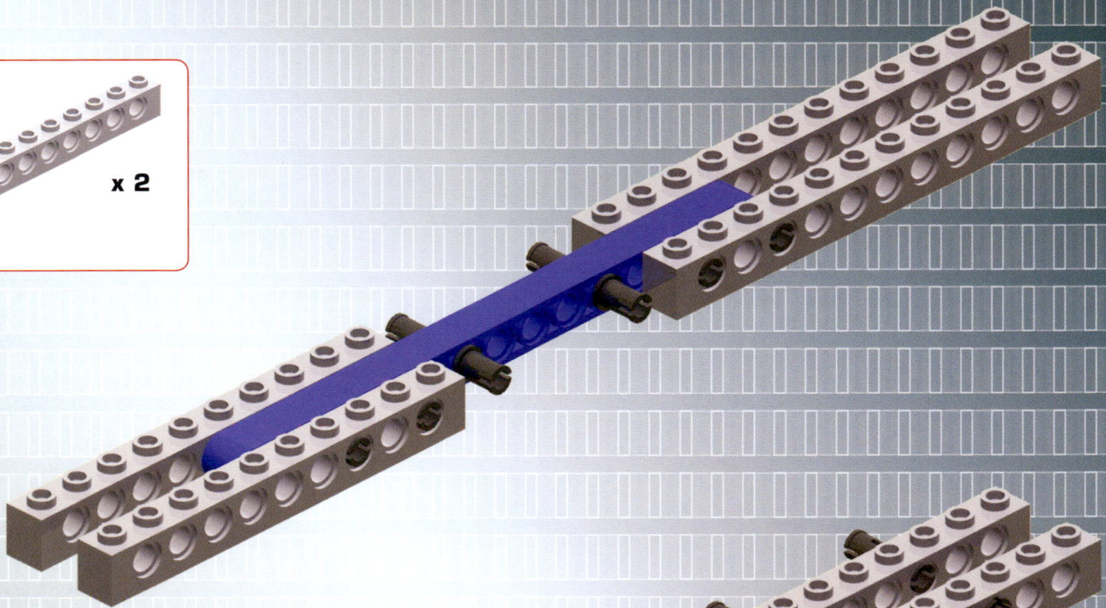

011

x 4

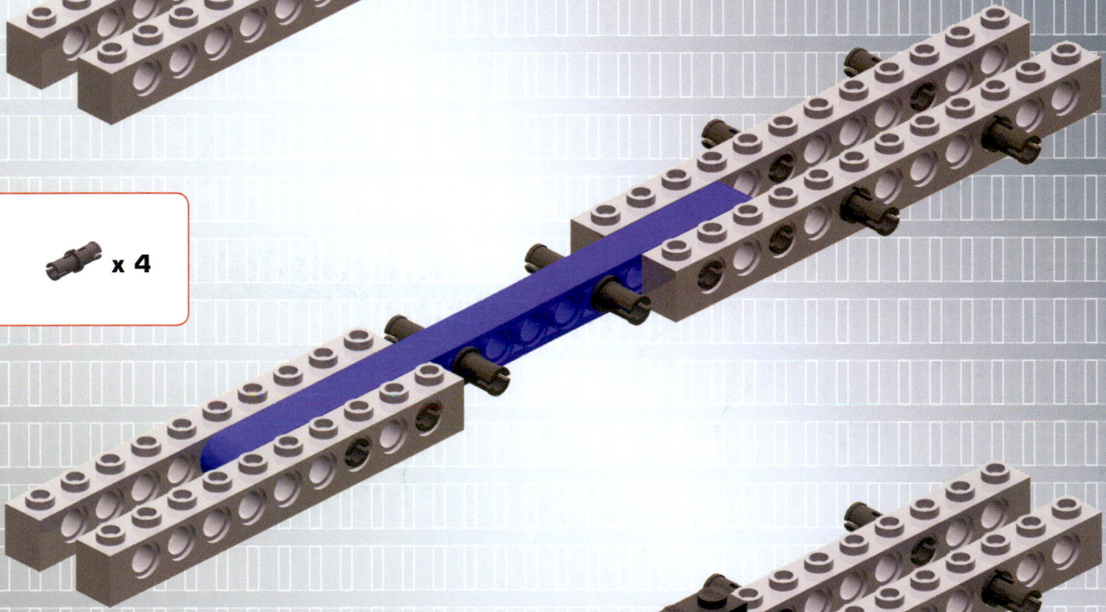

012

x 2

x 2

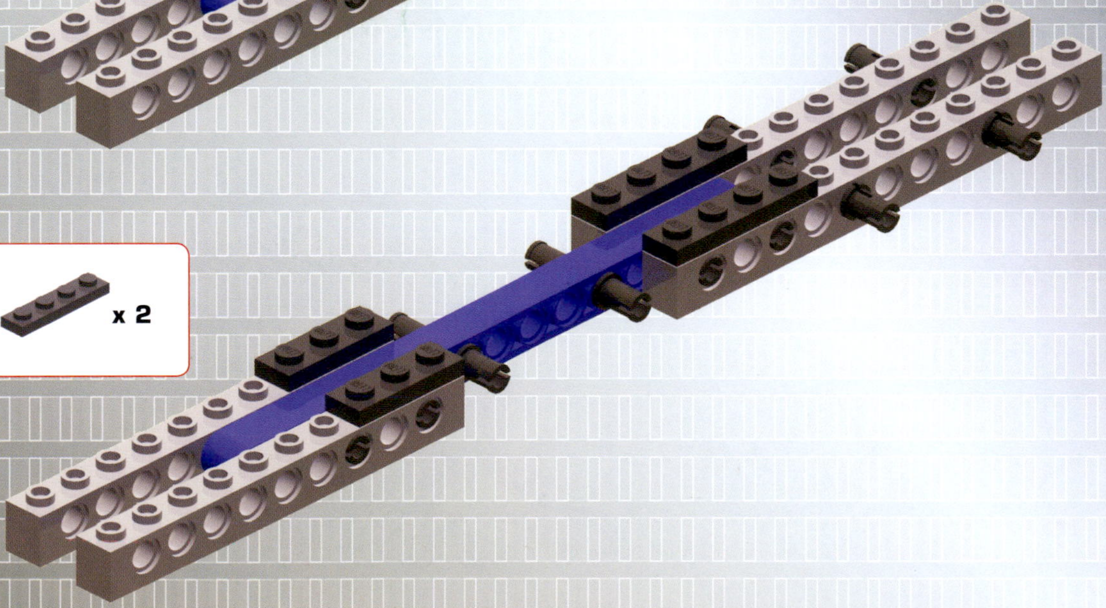

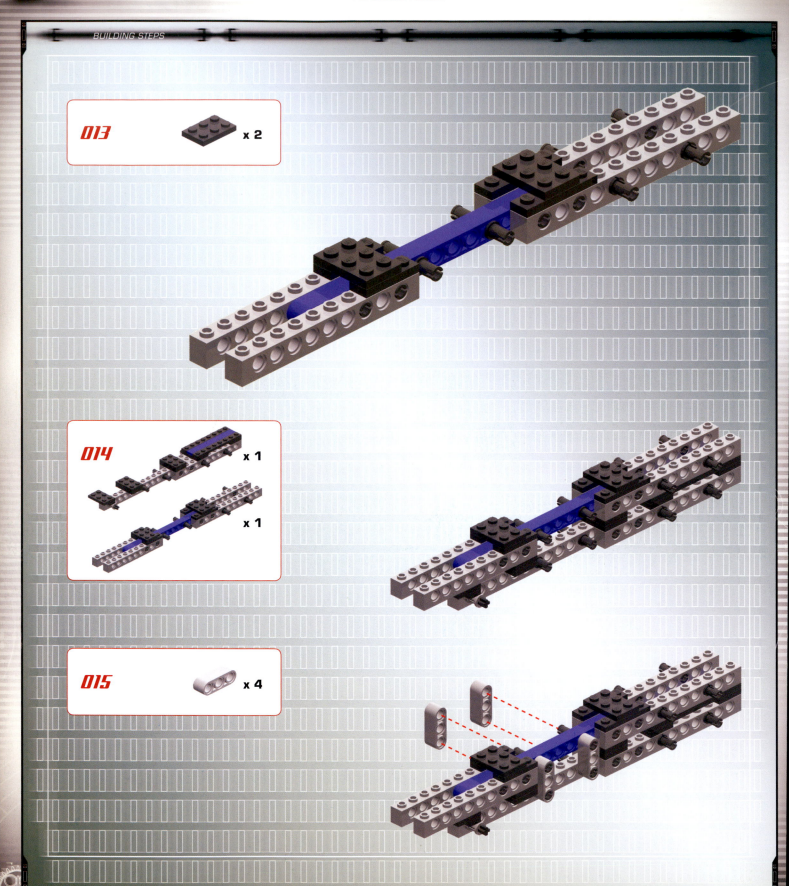

013 x 2

014 x 1
x 1

015 x 4

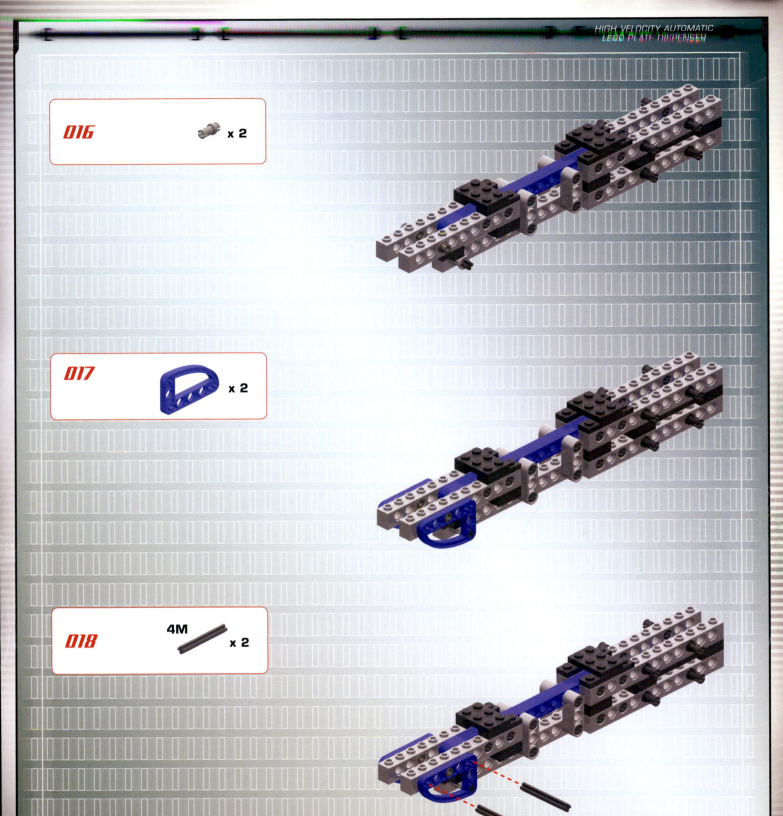

016 x 2

017 x 2

018 4M x 2

019 x 2

020 x 2

021 x 2
x 2

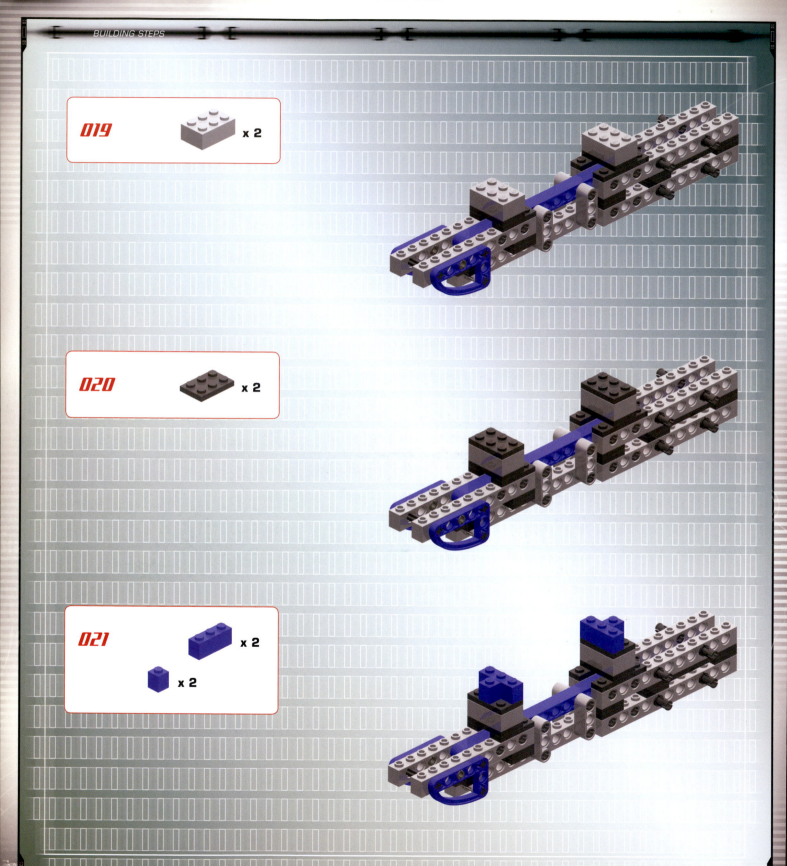

022

 x 2

x 2

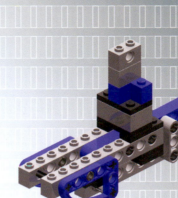

023

3M x 2

x 1

024

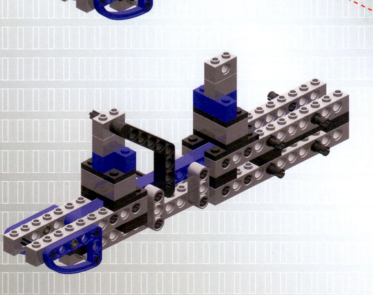

025

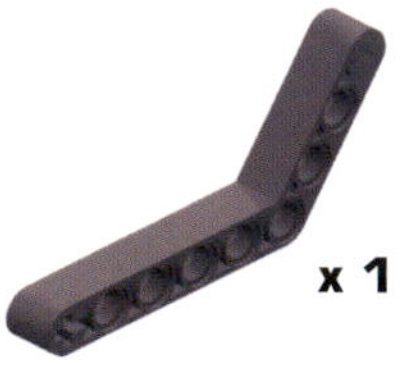

x 1

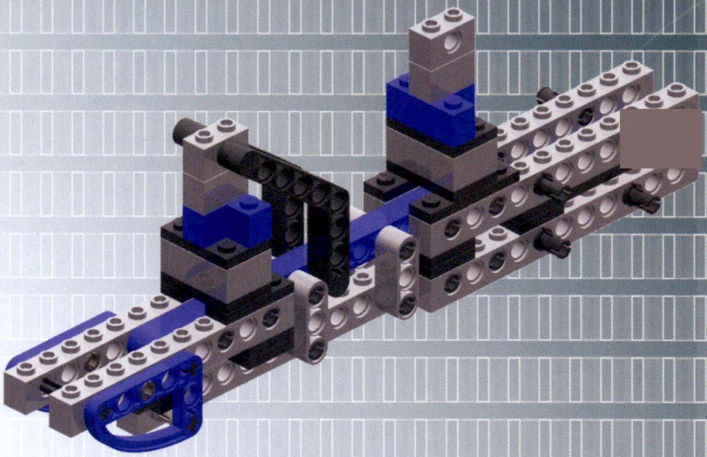

026

3M

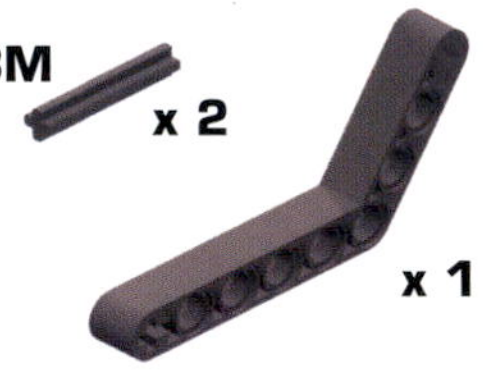

x 2

x 1

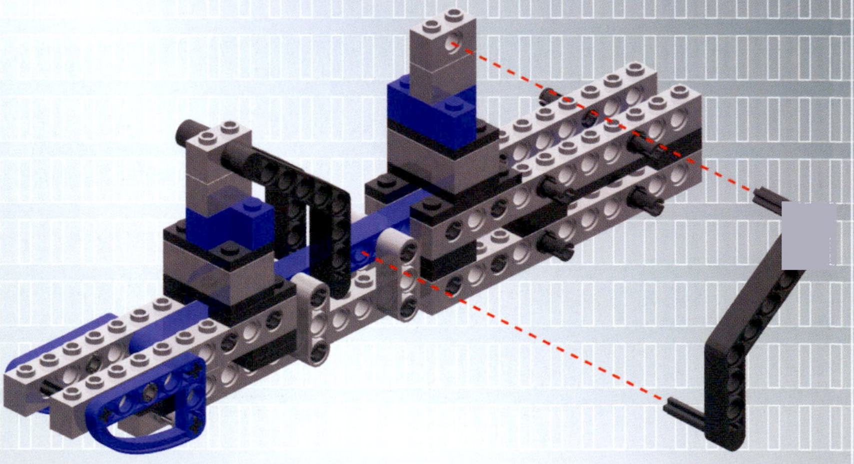

027

028

x 1

029

x 4

030

 x 2

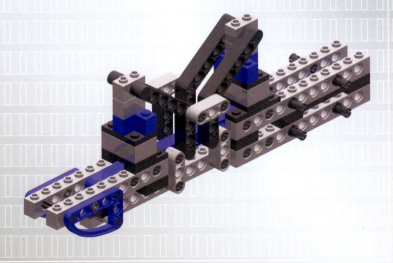

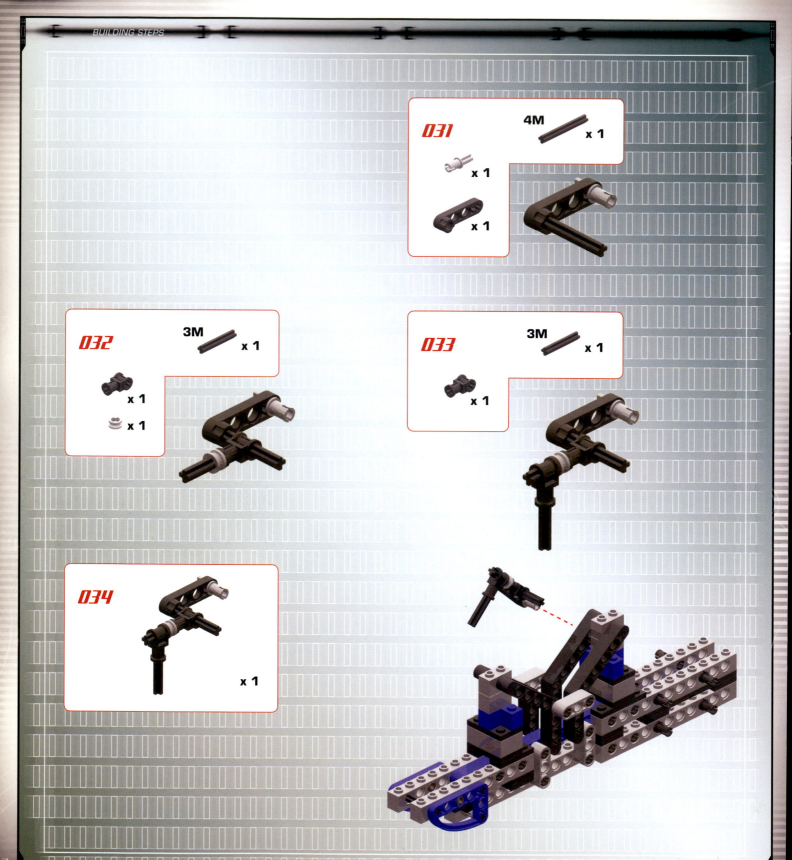

031 4M x 1
x 1
x 1

032 3M x 1
x 1
x 1

033 3M x 1
x 1

034 x 1

035

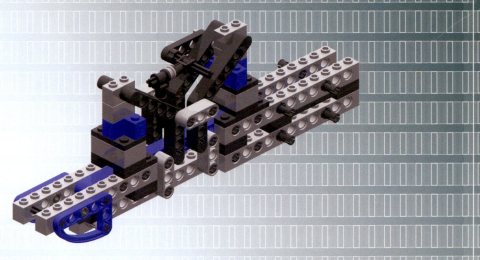

036

x 1

x 1

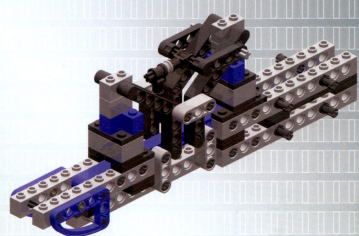

037

x 1

x 1

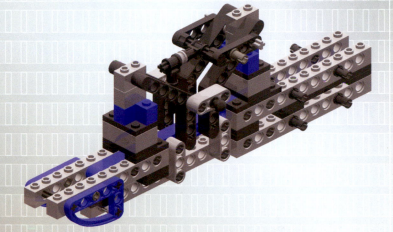

038

x 1

x 2

x 1

039

x 1

x 1

040

x 1

x 1

041

x 1

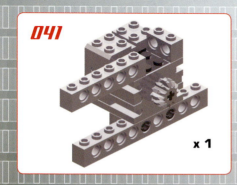

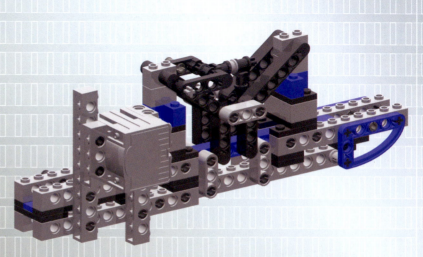

042

5M x 1

x 2

x 1*

* USE THE CUT
GEAR WHEEL

043

x 1

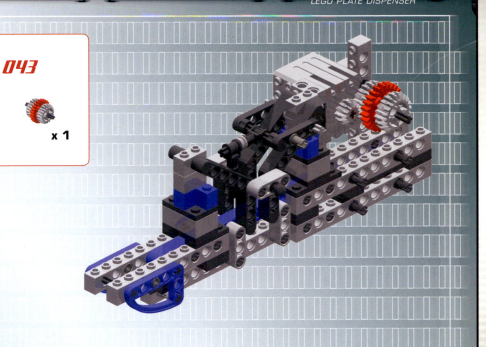

044

x 2

x 1

x 1

045

x 1

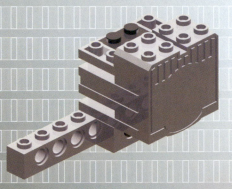

046

x 1

047

x 1

x 1

048

x 1

049

x 2

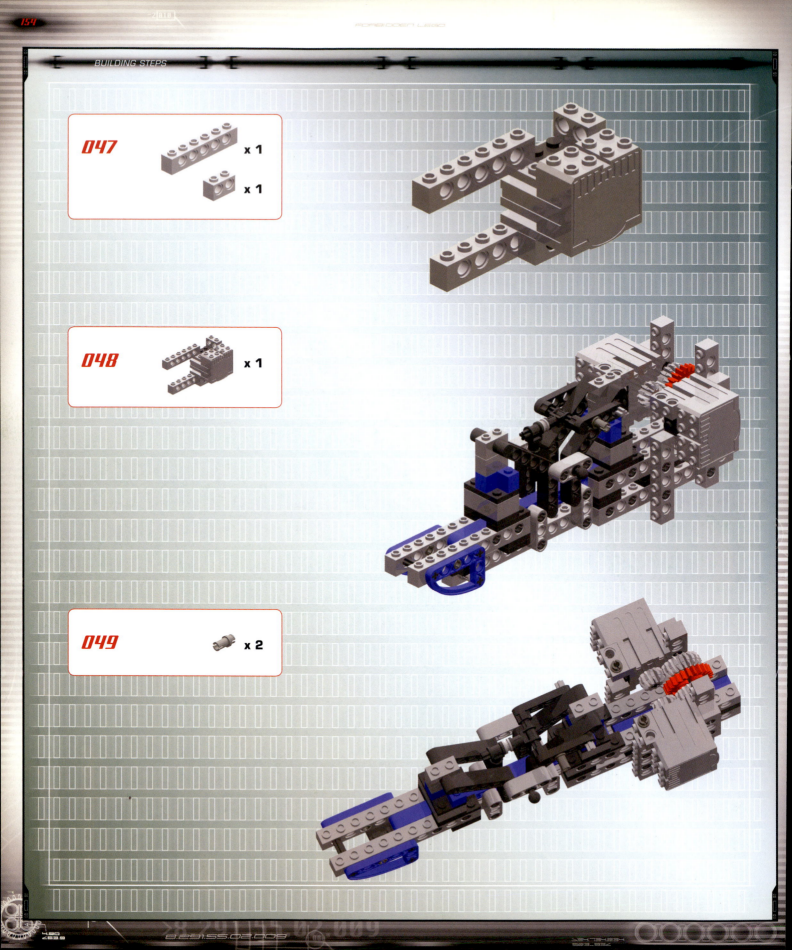

050 x 1

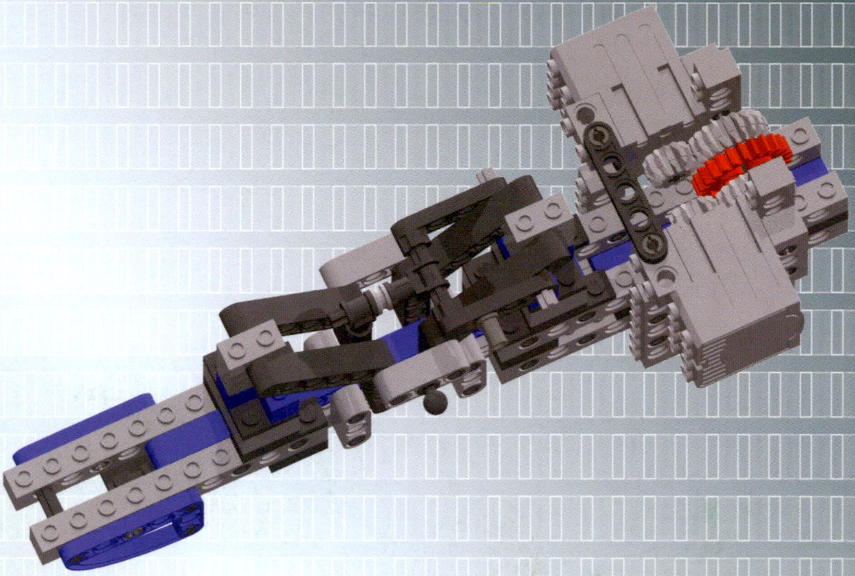

051  x 2

052 x 2

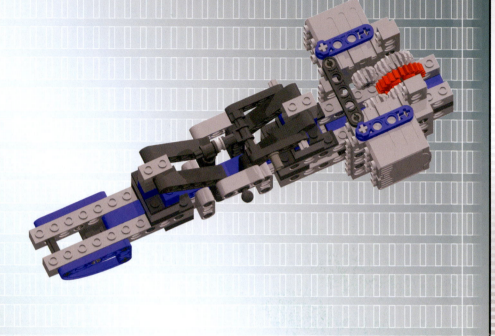

053 2M x 2

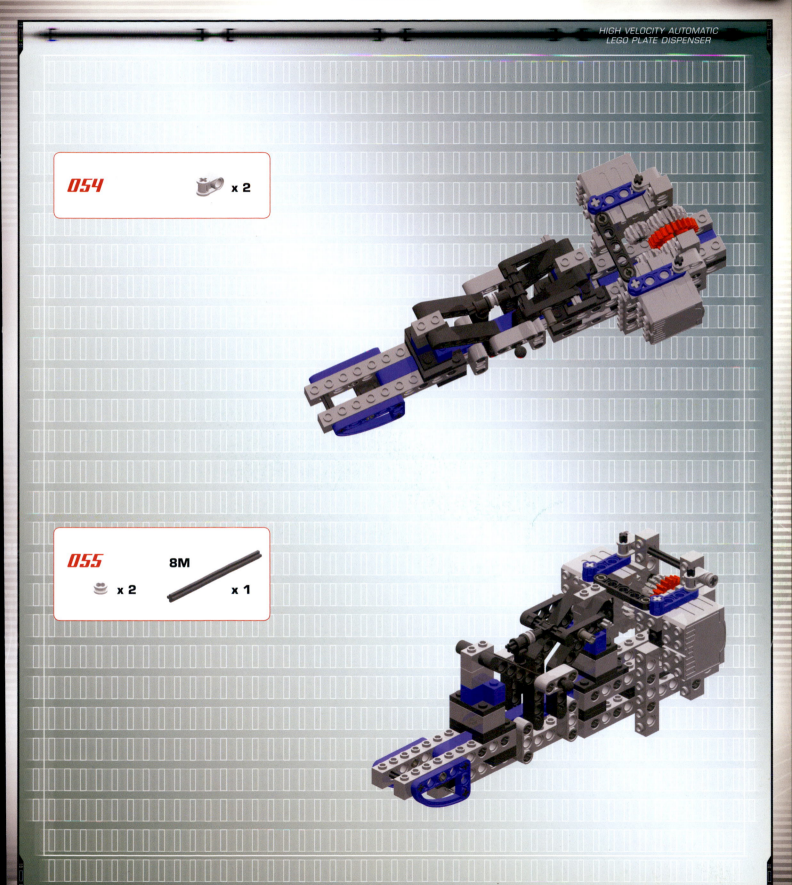

054 ✖ x 2

055 8M x 2 x 1

056 x 1

Insert the assembly that you created from the Tip instructions at the beginning of this project.

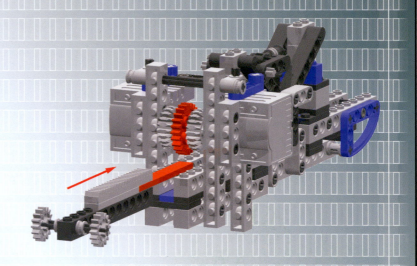

057

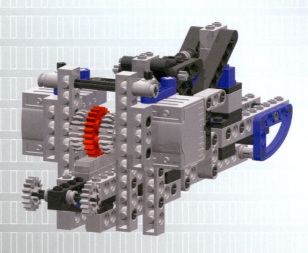

058

x 2

059
5M

x 1

x 1

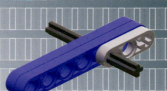

060
6M

x 1

x 1

061
x 2

062
x 2

x 2

063

x 2

064

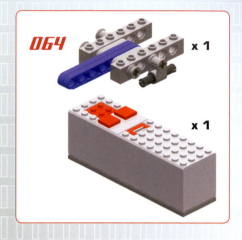

x 1

x 1

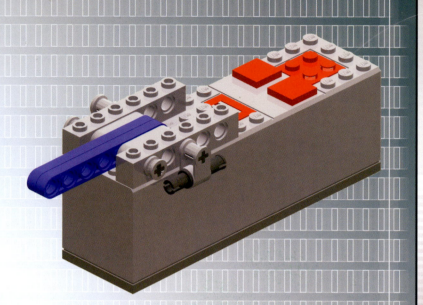

065

x 2

x 2

066

x 2

067 8M  x 2

068  x 2

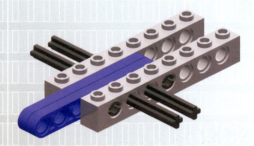

069 x 2

070 x 4

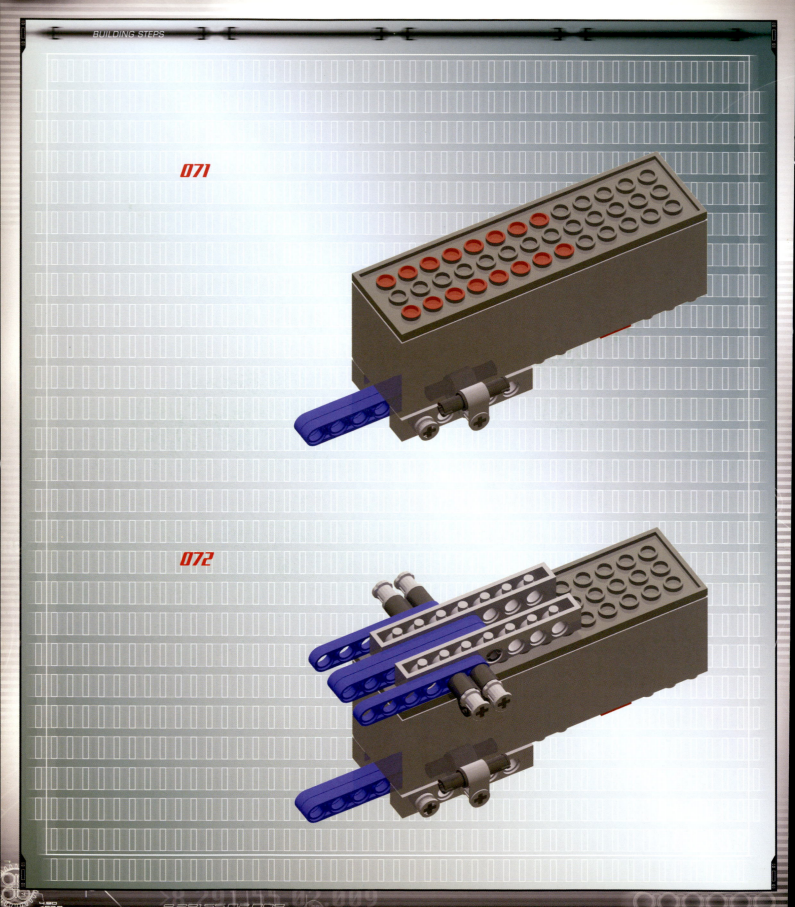

071

072

073

 x 2

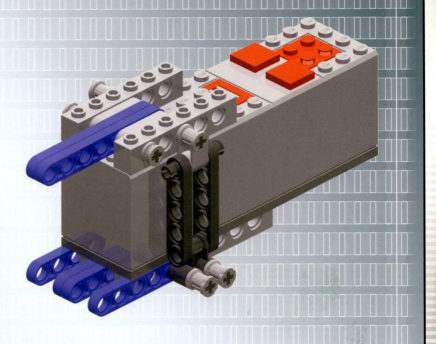

074

3M  x 1

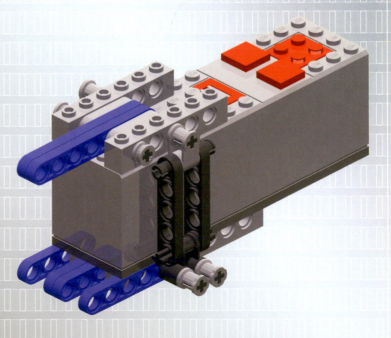

075   x 2

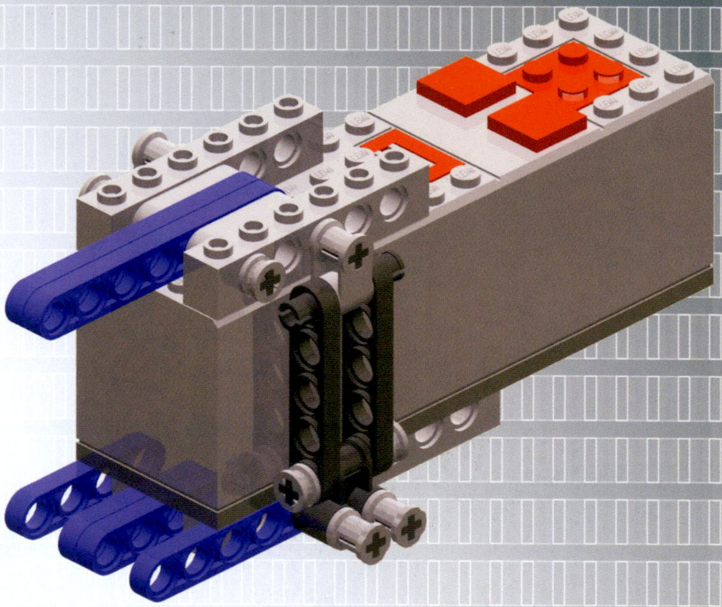

076   x 2

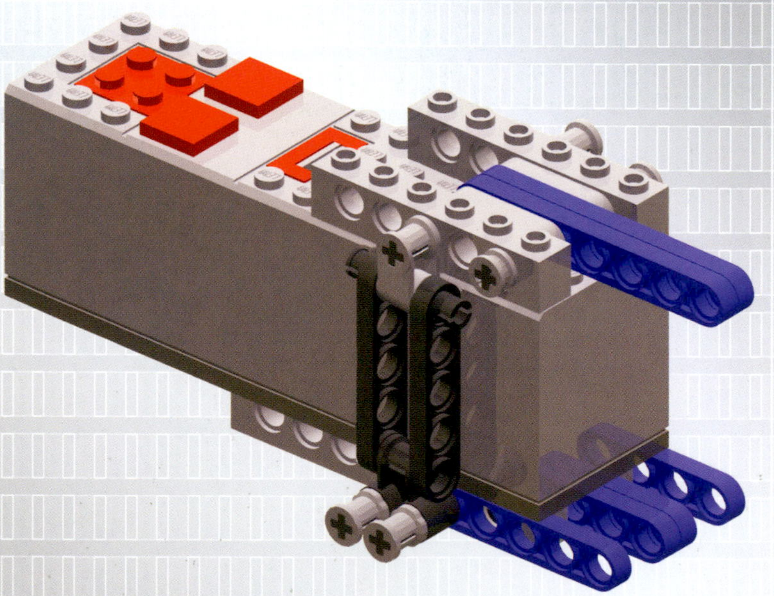

077 3M ⬛ x 1

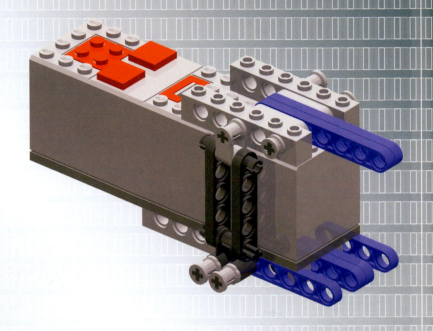

078 ⬤ x 2

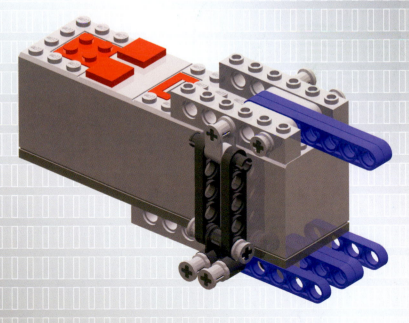

079

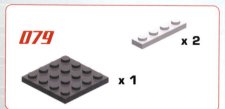

x 2

x 1

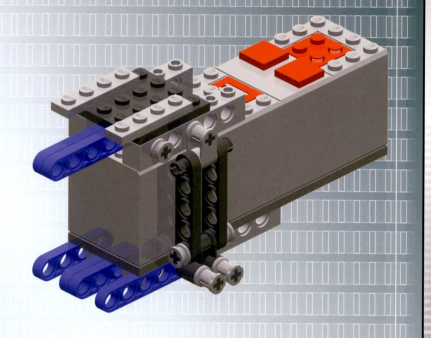

080

x 1

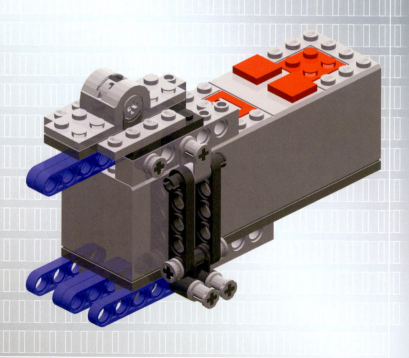

081

3M x 1 x 1 x 1

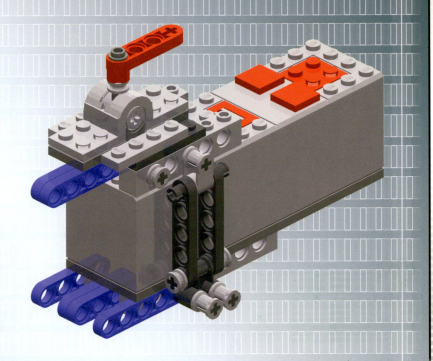

082

5M x 1 x 2

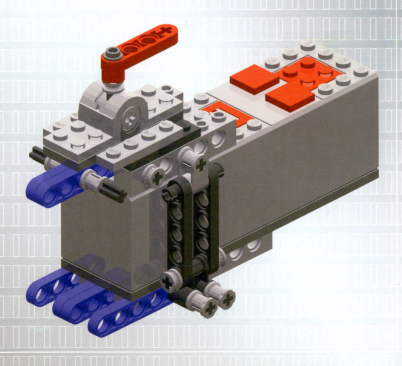

083   2M   x 2

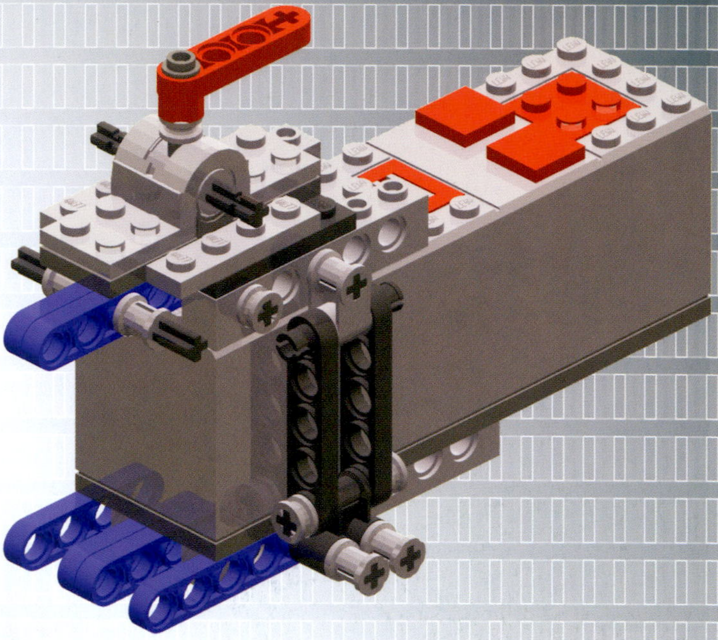

084   x 2

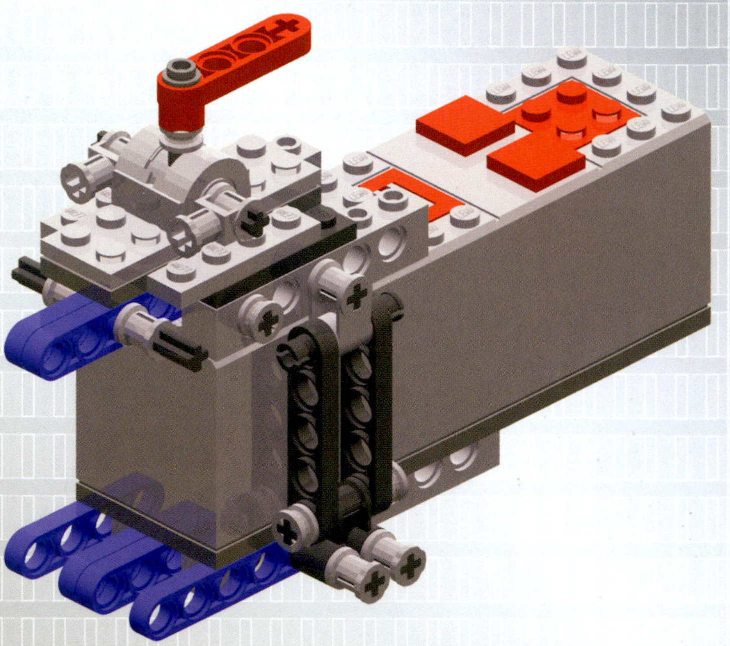

085   **2M**   x 2

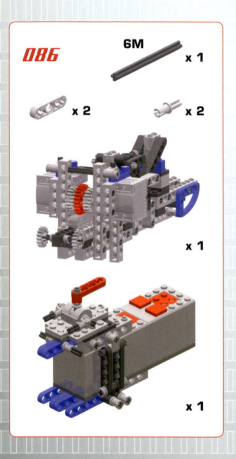

086

6M x 1

x 2   x 2

x 1

x 1

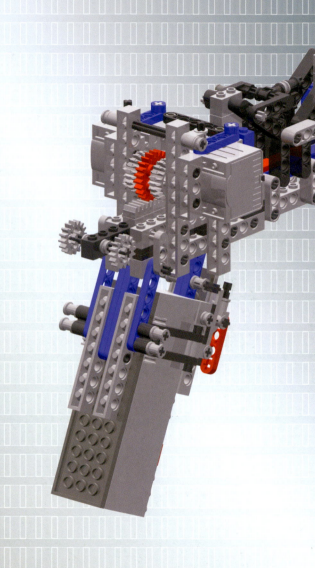

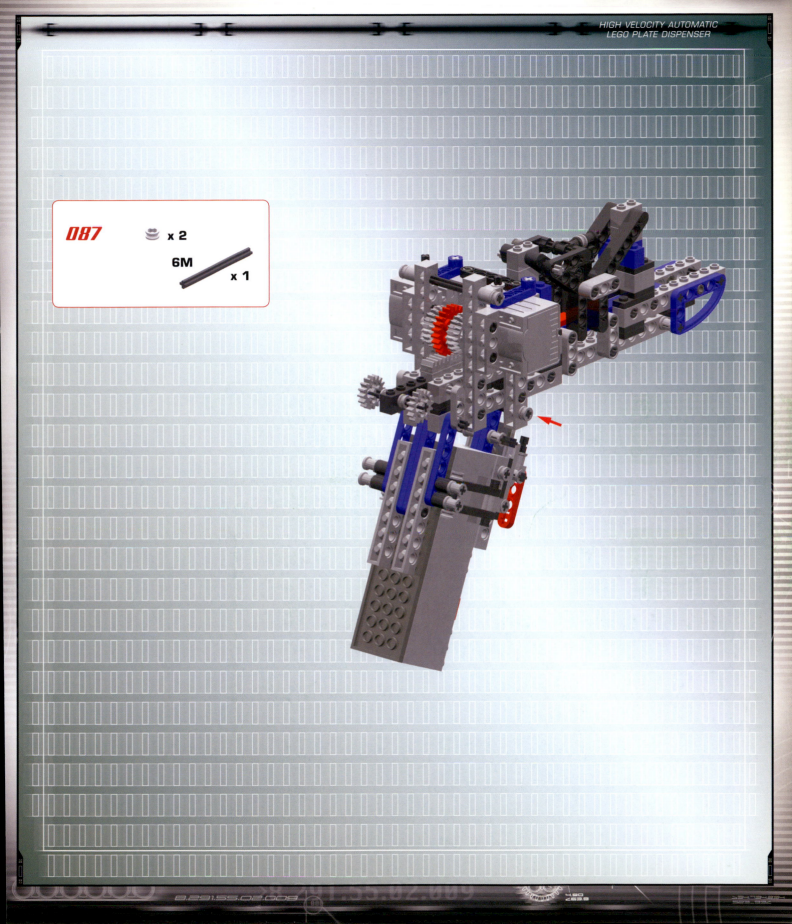

087   x 2

6M   x 1

088

x 1

089

x 1

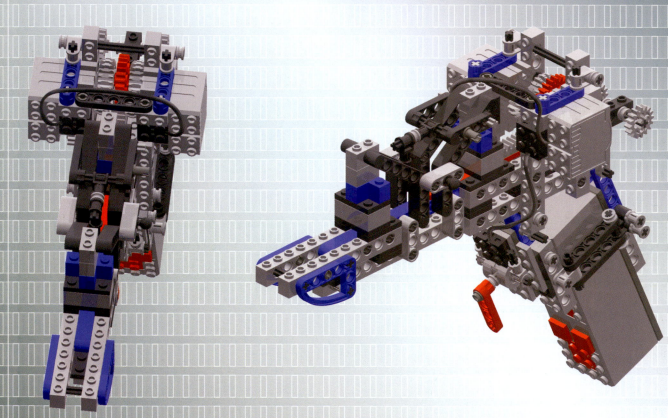

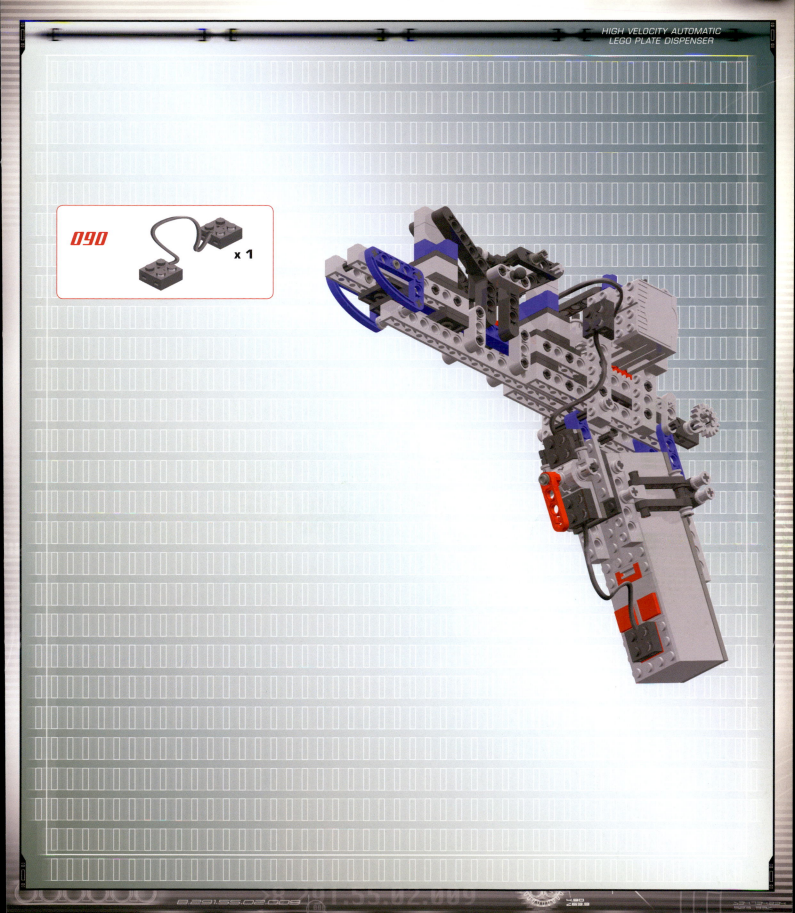

091

Remove liftarms from both sides to attach
rubber bands, as shown.

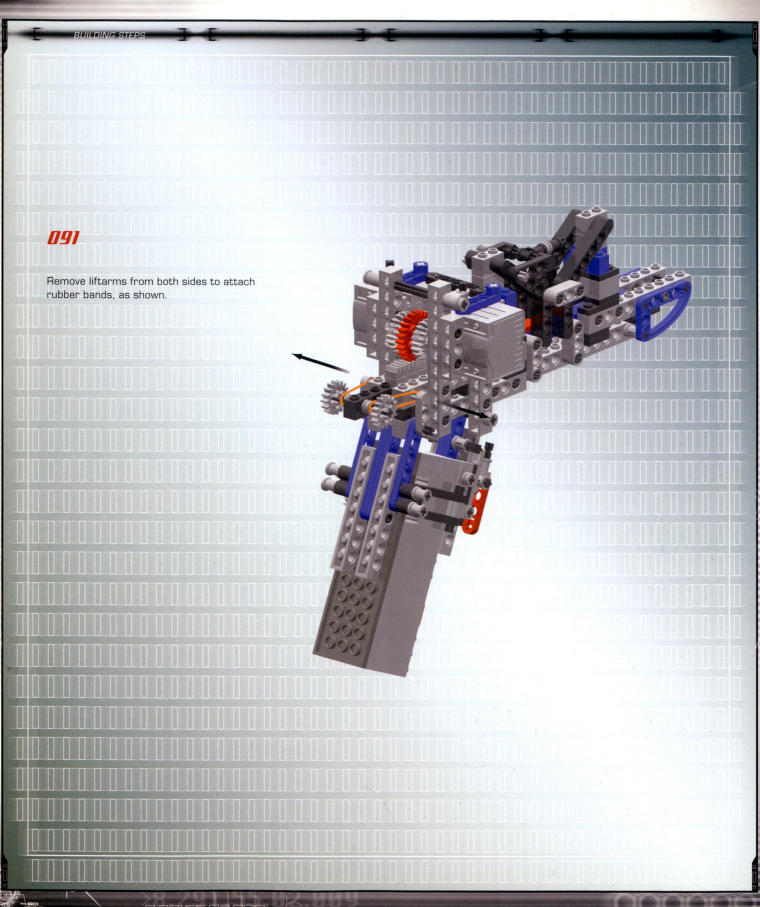

092

Attach rubber bands on both sides of the trigger, as shown. Also, mount a rubber band on the magazine pin on the top of the model.

093

Add up to 14 1 x 8 plates in the magazine.

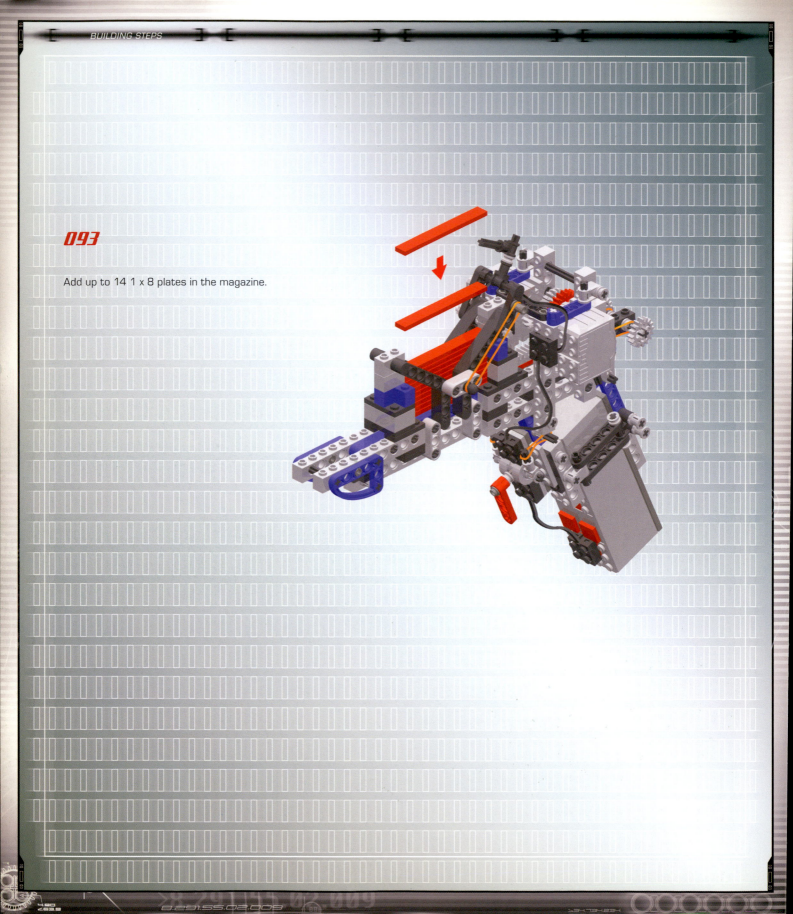

APPENDIX A:
TIPS AND TRICKS

18V MOTOR

Here's how you get 18V out of two LEGO 9V battery boxes and three LEGO wires. Attach the wires as shown in the instructions and enjoy full speed on all your creations! This trick will especially enhance the ATL and HVALPD projects.

001

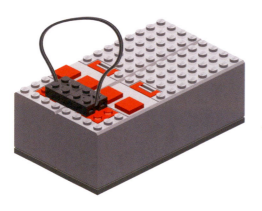

002

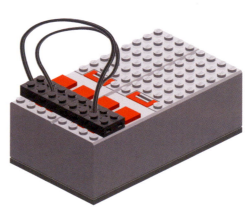

003

HAND-POWERED GENERATOR

Go green with this hand-cranked generator
that uses a regular LEGO TECHNIC motor
geared up three-to-one to generate enough
power to drive another motor in low speed
applications. This trick will work very well with
the CCC project.

001

002

003

NOTES: